LANCASTER PAMPHLETS

Democracy and Civil War in Spain 1931–1939

Martin Blinkhorn

ROUTLEDGE · LONDON

First published in 1988 by
Routledge
11 New Fetter Lane,
London, EC4P 4EE

© *1988 Martin Blinkhorn*

Filmset in Great Britain by
Mayhew Typesetting, Bristol
and printed in Great Britain
by Richard Clay Ltd, Bungay, Suffolk.

British Library Cataloguing in Publication
Data
Blinkhorn, Martin
Democracy and civil war in Spain
1931–1939. — (Lancaster pamphlets).
1. Spain — History — Republic,
1931–1939
I. Title   II. Series
946.081   DP254

ISBN 0-415-00699-6

Contents

Foreword

Lancaster Pamphlets offer concise and up-to-date accounts of major historical topics, primarily for the help of students preparing for Advanced Level examinations, though they should also be of value to those pursuing introductory courses in universities and other institutions of higher education. Without being all-embracing, their aims are to bring some of the central themes or problems confronting students and teachers into sharper focus than the textbook writer can hope to do; to provide the reader with some of the results of recent research which the textbook may not embody; and to stimulate thought about the whole interpretation of the topic under discussion.

At the end of this pamphlet is a list of works, most of them recent or fairly recent, which the writer considers most important for those who wish to study the subject further.

Acknowledgements

I should like to express my sincere gratitude to the two editors of the Lancaster Pamphlets, my colleagues Eric Evans and David King, for their helpful comments on the first draft of this pamphlet; to the many Lancaster students who through their interest in Spanish history have enabled me constantly to renew my own; and above all to my wife, Irene, and my daughter, Anna, for their unwavering support and understanding.

Chronological table of events

Before 1931

1873—4	First Republic
1875—1923	Constitutional Monarchy of Alfonso XII (d. 1885) and Alfonso XIII
1879	foundation of Spanish Socialist Party
1882	foundation of UGT
1898	Spanish—American War: loss of overseas empire
1910—11	foundation of CNT
1917	summer of political and constitutional crisis
1918—23	social unrest in Barcelona and Andalusia
1921	Spanish defeat in Morocco
1923	*coup d'état* of Primo de Rivera
1923—30	Primo de Rivera dictatorship
1930	fall of Primo de Rivera
1930—1	interim dictatorship of Berenguer and Aznar
1930	
August	Pact of San Sebastian (socialists adhere in October)
December	republican military revolt in Jaca
1931	
12 April	municipal elections
14 April	proclamation of Republic and flight of Alfonso XIII

The Second Republic 1931–6

1931
<table>
<tbody>
<tr><td>April–June</td><td>decrees on wages, rents, education etc.</td></tr>
<tr><td>May</td><td>church burnings</td></tr>
<tr><td>June</td><td>expulsion of Cardinal Segura
Constituent Cortes election</td></tr>
<tr><td>October</td><td>resignation of Alcalá Zamora and Maura; Azaña becomes Prime Minister</td></tr>
<tr><td>December</td><td>promulgation of Republican Constitution
Radicals leave government
foundation of JONS</td></tr>
</tbody>
</table>

1932
<table>
<tbody>
<tr><td>January</td><td>anarchist rising in Catalonia
Jesuits dissolved and other anticlerical measures enacted</td></tr>
<tr><td>August</td><td>Sanjurjo rising</td></tr>
<tr><td>September</td><td>Cortes approve Agrarian Reform Law and Statute of Catalan Autonomy</td></tr>
</tbody>
</table>

1933
<table>
<tbody>
<tr><td>January</td><td>anarchist rising; Casas Viejas incident</td></tr>
<tr><td>March</td><td>foundation of CEDA and Renovación Española</td></tr>
<tr><td>April</td><td>local elections: setback for governing coalition</td></tr>
<tr><td>September</td><td>Supreme Court elections: defeat for governmental candidates; resignation of Azaña</td></tr>
<tr><td>October</td><td>foundation of Falange</td></tr>
<tr><td>November</td><td>general election: defeat of left, victory of Radicals and CEDA, Lerroux Prime Minister</td></tr>
<tr><td>December</td><td>anarchist risings in Aragon, Catalonia and Rioja</td></tr>
</tbody>
</table>

1934
<table>
<tbody>
<tr><td>February</td><td>fusion of Falange and JONS</td></tr>
<tr><td>March</td><td>Salazar Alonso Minister of the Interior
Zaragoza general strike (CNT)
monarchist deputation to Mussolini</td></tr>
<tr><td>June</td><td>FNTT rural labourers' strike</td></tr>
<tr><td>October</td><td>CEDA enters government with three ministers; Asturias and Barcelona risings</td></tr>
</tbody>
</table>

1935
<table>
<tbody>
<tr><td>March</td><td>two more CEDA ministers in government</td></tr>
<tr><td>May</td><td>Gil Robles Minister of War</td></tr>
</tbody>
</table>

September	resignation of Lerroux
December	CEDA ousted from interim government
1936	
January	Popular Front electoral pact
February	election victory of Popular Front; Azaña government
March—April	fusion of Socialist and Communist Youth
May	Azaña President of the Republic; Casares Quiroga Prime Minister
May—June	Falangist-Socialist violence; widening divisions within Socialist Party
13 July	assassination of Calvo Sotelo
17—18 July	military rising

The Civil War

1936	
July	start of social revolution in Republican zone
	Germany and Italy commence aid to Nationalists
September	Largo Caballero government (joined by CNT in November)
	Irún, San Sebastián, Toledo fall to Nationalists
October	Franco becomes head of Nationalist State
	Soviet aid begins to reach Republic
November	Franco fails to take Madrid; Republican government moves to Valencia; arrival of International Brigades
1937	
February—March	Battles of Jarama and Guadalajara; Málaga falls to Nationalists
April	Franco unifies Falange and Carlists in FET
	Bombing of Guernica
May	Barcelona 'civil war within the Civil War'
	Fall of Largo Caballero and formation of Negrín government
June	Bilbao falls to Nationalists
July	Battle of Brunete
August	dissolution of Council of Aragon

August– October	fall of north coast to Nationalists
September	Battle of Belchite
October	Negrín government moves to Barcelona
December	Republicans capture Teruel
1938	
February	Nationalists recapture Teruel
April	Reorganization of Negrín government; resignation of Prieto
	Nationalists reach Mediterranean: Republican zone split into two
July– November	Battle of the Ebro: final Republican offensive
December	start of Nationalist advance into Catalonia
1939	
January– February	Nationalists occupy Catalonia
March	Casado coup in Republican zone
	Nationalists occupy Madrid and 'central zone'
1 April	Franco declares Civil War at an end

List of abbreviations used in the text

CEDA   *Confederación Española de Derechas Autónomas* (Spanish Confederation of Autonomous Right-wing Groups): conservative Catholic party under the Second Republic

CNCA   *Confederación Nacional Católico-Agraria* (National Catholic-Agrarian Confederation): Catholic landowners' and farmers' pressure group

CNT   *Confederación Nacional del Trabajo* (National Confederation of Labour): anarchist labour organization

FET   *Falange Española Tradicionalista y de las JONS*: single party of Nationalist Spain, formed in April 1937 out of fusion of Falange and Carlists (see JONS)

FNTT   *Federación Nacional de Trabajadores de la Tierra* (National Landworkers' Federation): socialist agricultural labourers' union

JONS   *Juntas de Ofensiva Nacional-Sindicalista* (National-Syndicalist Offensive Groups): fascist group formed in 1931 and fused in 1934 with Falange

PNV   *Partido Nacionalista Vasco* (Basque Nationalist Party)

POUM   *Partido Obrero de Unificación Marxista* (Workers' Party of Marxist Unification): small anti-Stalinist communist party, based in Catalonia

UGT   *Unión General de Trabajadores* (General Workers' Union): socialist trade-union organization

Maps

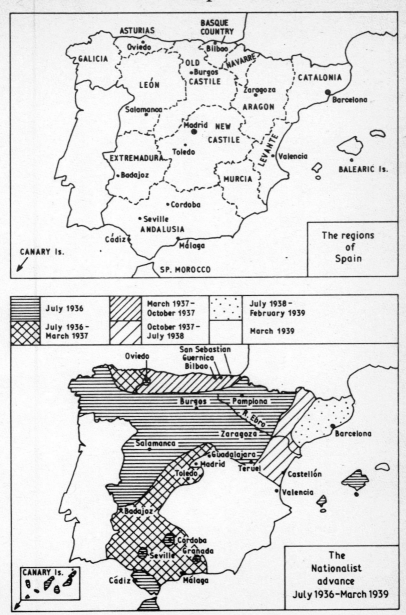

The regions
of
Spain

| July 1936 | March 1937–October 1937 | July 1938–February 1939 |
| July 1936–March 1937 | October 1937–July 1938 | March 1939 |

The
Nationalist
advance
July 1936–March 1939

Introduction

To the English-speaking world, the Spanish Civil War of 1936–9 is familiar nowadays chiefly through the poetry of W. H. Auden, George Orwell's classic war memoir *Homage to Catalonia* and, most of all perhaps, Ernest Hemingway's novel *For Whom the Bell Tolls*. This alone testifies to the passions that the war aroused among non-Spanish contemporaries, for many of whom its significance went well beyond Spain itself. Thousands of foreigners from all parts of the world were so concerned about events in Spain that they actually went there to fight in the war, many of them never to return. For most of these volunteers the war represented a kind of crusade against the greatest evil of the day: fascism, as represented by General Franco's Nationalist rebels and their Italian and German allies. Helping the young Spanish Republic in its struggle for survival against these powerful enemies was, or seemed to be, a way of resisting the advance of a sinister creed and political system which threatened to engulf the whole of Europe. Not all foreigners sympathized with the Republic, however. A smaller number volunteered to assist the rebels, likewise out of a conviction that on Spanish soil a wider struggle was being fought out. For them too — and for the Nationalists themselves, who adopted the term officially — this was a crusade, but one on behalf of Christianity against godless 'Bolshevism' as incarnate in the Republic's left-wing allies and Soviet backers.

It is quite understandable that contemporaries, whatever their sympathies, should have viewed the Spanish Civil War in such cosmic terms. Whilst the confrontation between the Spanish Republic and its right-wing opponents may have differed in significant respects from the events surrounding the death of democracy in, for example, Italy, Germany and Austria — not least because in Spain there *was* a three-year civil war — the underlying similarities were real enough. It is nevertheless important to recognize that the conflict was in no serious sense the *product* of forces extraneous to Spain. The Spanish Civil War, in origin and essence, was precisely that: a civil war arising out of Spanish conditions and, notwithstanding the foreign contribution, fought overwhelmingly between Spaniards.

Political regimes may come and go; *coups d'état* may be commonplace; but major civil wars like that in Spain, involving hundreds of thousands of casualties, are mercifully rare. The Spanish crisis of the 1930s therefore presents the historian with fascinating and difficult questions. Why, for example, did the Spanish democracy born in 1931 not endure? What made it so difficult for Spaniards during the 1930s to coexist peacefully? Even given their failure to do so, why was the outcome a protracted civil war? Why did victory in the war go to Franco and the Nationalists? Were left-wing contemporaries correct in considering their enemies 'fascists'? These are among the questions that this pamphlet will attempt to tackle. First, however, we must examine how and why Spain became a democracy in 1931.

1

From monarchy to Republic

In 1898 Spain suffered at the hands of the upstart United States a humiliating military and naval defeat in the Caribbean and Pacific. Defeat was followed by a yet greater humiliation: Spain's loss of the final remnants — Cuba, Puerto Rico and the Philippines — of a vast overseas empire, conquered during the sixteenth century and still intact as late as the early nineteenth. The material loss suffered in the 'Disaster of 1898' was significant, but the psychological blow was even greater. As Spaniards came face to face with their country's impotence, backwardness and inescapably second-class status, there arose a confused chorus of demands for the 'regeneration' of what was widely seen as a 'decadent' nation. For the Spanish monarchy, 1898 signalled the start of a lengthy process of disintegration which culminated in 1931 with its replacement by the Second Republic.

The old regime

Decadent or not, Spain in the early twentieth century was certainly backward in relation to other European states: not merely Britain, Germany and France but also the more obviously comparable Italy. One measure of this was the overwhelmingly rural-agrarian character of her economy and society. Even by 1930, 46 per cent of the active population was still directly involved in agriculture, and at least another 10 per cent in essentially rural industries. Truly 'modern' industry was largely restricted to the northern periphery — the textile factories of Catalonia and the iron, steel, shipbuilding and paper industries of the Basque country. Only here, and in mining districts like Asturias, could there be said to exist a modern bourgeoisie and an industrial working class. Elsewhere, Spain's was not only an agrarian economy but also a very retarded and unproductive one, upon which was founded an often staggeringly unjust society. Of Spain's complex agrarian problems, two are of particular importance to us. Characteristic of large areas of southern Spain, notably the regions of Andalusia, Extremadura and La Mancha, were the vast private estates or *latifundios*, often owned by absentee proprietors and usually worked by armies of desperately impoverished landless labourers. In many other regions, especially north of Madrid, peasant farming was more typical; here the small farmer, either as proprietor or tenant, struggled under the burden of such problems as poor soil, debt, tiny and often scattered holdings, unavailable or expensive credit, high rents and insecure leases. Not surprisingly, rural unrest, frequently suppressed by the ruthless Civil Guard, was a chronic feature of Spanish life, and the 'agrarian question' a major concern of those who sought to make Spain more modern and democratic.

Would-be reformers were also preoccupied by two powerful institutions which seemed to epitomize and reinforce Spain's general backwardness. The Spanish Church, although forced by nineteenth-century liberal governments to release most of its vast landed wealth, remained during the early twentieth century a rich, powerful and traditionalist institution whose ties with the wealthy classes, moreover, were becoming closer. Through its near monopoly of education the Church instilled into those who did not rebel against it a profoundly conservative system of religious, social and political values. The second institutional prop of conservative Spain was the army: an absurdly over-officered and militarily inefficient body, acutely sensitive to criticism and, after 1900, increasingly inclined towards interfering in politics.

Over Spain's stuttering economy and unequal society there presided the so-called 'Liberal Monarchy'. Introduced in 1875 following seven years of political and social instability, this regime brought a generation of political peace based upon the dominance of big landowners, especially the landlords of Castile and the 'latifundists' of Andalusia. By the turn of the century the landed class had been joined in a powerful ruling oligarchy by the representatives of 'new' economic forces, principally the bankers and heavy industrialists of the Basque country and the manufacturers of Catalonia. Political stability was ensured by a superficially representative electoral system — Spain received universal manhood suffrage in 1887 — which in reality was far from democratic. By subjecting voters to a combination of bribery, economic pressure and downright coercion, the Ministry of the Interior and, at local level, *caciques* — bigwigs and political 'bosses' — constructed pre-arranged governmental majorities for one or other of the two main 'oligarchic' parties, the Liberals and the Conservatives. For many who in the early twentieth century longed for the 'regeneration' of Spain, the phrase 'oligarchy and *caciquismo*' summed up the country's ills.

The crisis of the monarchy

Between 1898 and 1923 the development of a more complex and less easily controlled society confronted the monarchy of King Alfonso XIII with a series of new challenges. Educated, urban Spaniards demanded institutional and constitutional reforms, some going so far as to favour the monarchy's replacement by a republic; in Catalonia and the Basque country, where distinctive languages and cultures existed, rising nationalist movements opposed the regime's centralizing character; in Morocco, Spain and her army became embroiled in what was to be her last colonial war; and two mass forces of the left, socialism and anarchism, emerged to offer organized protest against the injustices of Spanish society. As time passed and urban politics, at least, became more open and genuinely representative, the old, artificial party system began to crumble and the Liberal Monarchy itself to appear insecure. In a major crisis in the summer of 1917, some historians believe, only divisions between its middle-class and left-wing critics rescued the crown from a fate similar to that which only months before had befallen Tsar Nicolas II of Russia. The immediate crisis passed, but during the next six years the monarchy's problems if anything intensified, with military humiliation in Morocco and social unrest raging in the emerging anarchist strongholds of urban Catalonia and rural Andalusia: all this against a background of chronic governmental instability. By the early 1920s it was evident that the monarchical system in its existing form was ill-equipped to negotiate successfully the difficult transition from 'oligarchic' liberalism to genuine democracy.

The life of the Liberal Monarchy effectively ended in September 1923 with the military *pronunciamiento* (*coup d'état*) of General Miguel Primo de Rivera. With the King's acquiescence and in total contravention of the monarchy's constitution, Primo de Rivera proceeded to establish a dictatorship. While this may have appeared to solve the monarchy's immediate problems, in the long run it only made them worse. After an early honeymoon period during which he drove underground the anarchist trade union, the CNT, suppressed Catalan nationalism, brought peace to Morocco, and benefited from a shortlived economic boom, Primo de Rivera's credit gradually exhausted itself. In the face of rising popular hostility, and abandoned during the late 1920s by most of his powerful allies — the wealthy classes, his military colleagues and, crucially, Alfonso XIII himself — the dictator surrendered power in January 1930, bequeathing to the King the task of determining Spain's future constitutional course. During the next twelve months Alfonso entrusted the premiership first to another general, Berenguer, and then to an admiral, Aznar, each governing without parliamentary restraint. It was becoming increasingly clear, however, that continued recourse to dictatorship offered no lasting solution and that a return to representative politics would somehow have to be contrived.

This would not be easy, for beneath the surface of the dictatorship Spanish politics had been undergoing a dramatic transformation. The old Liberal and Conservative parties, moribund even before 1923, failed to re-emerge in recognizable and credible form in 1930. Nevertheless they had not yet been superseded by new organizations capable of combining loyalty to the monarchy with the representation of the socially and economically powerful. Ironically, moreover, the dictatorship, while accelerating the inexorable demise of the 'oligarchic' party system, had stimulated the growth of socialism and republicanism. The Spanish Socialist Party and its trade union organization, the UGT (General Workers' Union), had gained strength both from initially co-operating with the dictatorship and from subsequently opposing it. The rise of republicanism was if anything even more dramatic. A cause in the doldrums following the chaotic experience of the First Republic in 1873, republicanism had begun to revive after 1900, especially in the big cities. Alfonso XIII's complicity in the dictatorship and undermining of the monarchy's own constitution tarnished the very principle of monarchy and gave republicanism a tremendous boost, especially once Primo de Rivera's early popularity had deserted him. During the late 1920s republican ranks swelled not only with members of an expanding, educated urban middle class but also with recently active monarchists. For most of the former, republicanism involved a commitment to fundamentally reforming Spanish society; for many of the latter, little more than a conviction that a republic, if politically moderate, might prove a sounder guarantor of conservative interests than a discredited monarchy susceptible to outright revolution.

As the King and his ministers struggled to escape the constitutional impasse, the seriousness of the republican challenge became daily more evident. In August 1930 representatives of republican organizations signed a pact at San Sebastián aimed at overthrowing the monarchy; in October the Spanish Socialist Party joined the republicans in a 'Revolutionary Committee'; and in December a premature and unsuccessful rising of pro-republican army officers in Jaca (Aragon) provided the cause with its first 'martyrs'. Fearing further unrest Alfonso's government accepted the need for an electoral strategy and called local elections as the first stage in a gradual return to representative politics. Held on 12 April 1931 the contest turned into a more-or-less direct confrontation between monarchists and an alliance of republicans and socialists. In the countryside comfortable monarchist victories were achieved through the continuing social and political grip of *caciquismo*, but in the great majority of cities and large towns, where voting was freer, the triumph of the monarchy's opponents was resounding. To the King and most of his advisers the verdict was clear and, short of risking civil war, irresistible. On 14 April 1931, as Alfonso XIII prepared his departure from Spain, the Revolutionary Committee assumed office as the Provisional Government of the Second Republic.

7

2

The Second Republic and
the coming of civil war, 1931—6

Political and social forces

The Provisional Government, having assumed power in extra-
ordinary circumstances, lacked strict democratic legitimacy until a
general election could take place. The first of the Second Republic's
three general elections was held in late June 1931. In order to
weaken *caciquismo* and encourage broad political alliances, multi-
member constituencies and a new voting system were introduced.
The contest produced a 'Constituent' parliament (Sp. *Cortes*) overwhelmingly dominated by parties sympathetic to the new regime.
Out of 470 seats the Socialists won 113, the Radicals 89, the
Republican Left 85, the Catalonian and Galician allies of the latter
55, and other assorted pro-republicans around 60. In part this
dramatic result reflected a widespread but not necessarily depend-
able willingness to give the Republic a chance, in part the
temporary demoralization and organizational unpreparedness of
the anti- and non-republican right, whose fifty or so deputies
seriously under-represented its true strength and potential.

Between 14 April 1931 and September 1933, Spain was
governed by a succession of governments made up of Republicans
and Socialists. Until late 1931 all forces favourable to the new
regime were represented in government, ranging from the Socialist
Party, through an assortment of Left-Republican parties, to the

increasingly conservative Radical Party and the Catholic Republicans on the right. With the resignation of Catholic ministers in October 1931 and the shift into opposition of the Radicals two months later, power reverted to a coalition of Left-Republicans and Socialists led by the Republic's strongman, Manuel Azaña.

REPUBLICANISM AND THE SPANISH MIDDLE CLASS

The coming of the Republic was not a 'bourgeois revolution' involving the seizure of political power by representatives of a 'progressive', entrepreneurial middle class. Spain's financial and industrial bourgeoisie had decades before 1931 thrown in its lot with the monarchy and the landed class; as an immediate and massive flight of capital indicated, business interests substantially shared the suspicion, if not downright hostility, with which large landowners from the outset regarded the new regime. Most of the Republican politicians who assumed office in April 1931 represented instead that professional middle class and intelligentsia — lawyers and bureaucrats; literati and journalists; academics and schoolteachers; doctors, dentists and vets — which had largely abandoned the monarchy during the 1920s. Although in an economically backward country like Spain these elements played an important cultural role, they lacked economic 'muscle', a weakness that was accordingly transmitted to the Republic itself.

As a predominantly middle-class cause, Spanish republicanism, and in particular its more reform-minded elements, suffered from the lack of a truly broad popular base, comparable with that enjoyed by French republicanism, within a numerous and vigorous lower-middle class and peasantry. Throughout much of urban Spain the lower-middle class, whilst larger than is sometimes suggested, was engaged in relatively small-scale economic activities involving little in the way of enterprise: family-based manufacturing, localized commerce, a primitive service sector, and not least important the buying, selling and leasing of land — a major middle-class preoccupation since the disentailment of the Church's landed property in the mid-nineteenth century. Although sections of this lower-middle class were progressively inclined and thus, initially at least, sympathetic towards the Republic, much of it remained highly traditionalist in outlook, devoutly Catholic, exaggeratedly status-conscious towards the working class, and bitterly hostile

9

towards anything which smacked even vaguely of 'socialism'. All this was even more true of the middling and lesser landowning and rent-paying peasantry, caught as many of its members were within a web of economic, cultural and ideological subjection to their social superiors and an authoritarian Church. Only in industrialized Catalonia, in Madrid, and to a lesser extent in other big cities like Valencia and Seville, did the makings of a genuine mass, lower-middle-class base for republicanism clearly exist in 1931.

As well as being deficient in mass support, the Republican politicians who numerically dominated the Provisional Government lacked unity amongst themselves. The provisional premier and future President of the Republic, Alcalá Zamora, and the Interior minister, Maura, were wealthy, Catholic ex-monarchists anxious to assuage conservative fears with a mildly reformist but politically moderate Republic. The radical Party, led by an elderly, reformed ex-demagogue, Alejandro Lerroux, was Spain's oldest surviving Republican party. By now Radical in name only, the party found its ambitions satisfied by the mere arrival of a Republic; forthwith it began to offer a refuge to former monarchists and adopt increasingly conservative positions on social issues. Left-republicanism was represented by a number of parties: the Catalan Left and the Galician autonomists, the Radical—Socialists and Azaña's Republican Action party. While differing over details of policy, the Left-Republican parties shared a common desire to liberate the minds of Spaniards from the centuries-old chains — as they saw it — of traditionalism and religious obscurantism. The result was an excessive emphasis on anticlericalism.

SOCIALISM AND ANARCHISM

From the outset their lack of an independent popular base forced Azaña and the Left-Republicans to lean for both electoral and parliamentary support upon the Socialist Party, which through the UGT was able during 1930—1 to mobilize on the Republic's behalf a large proportion of the Spanish working class. Until the 1930s the Socialist Party, its Marxist programme notwithstanding, had been generally cautious and reformist, while the UGT, strongest in Madrid, the Basque country and the mining region of Asturias, had traditionally been an organization of moderate skilled workers. From 14 April 1931 down to September 1933 the Socialists held three ministerial portfolios: Indalecio Prieto occupied the Finance ministry in the Provisional Government and later the Ministry of Public Works; Fernando de los Ríos was Minister of Justice; and the Ministry of Labour was occupied throughout by the general secretary of the UGT, Francisco Largo Caballero, a former plasterer who had left school at seven and was later to be Prime Minister of the wartime Republic.

Socialists differed among themselves over how far their party's commitment to the Republic should go, some looking merely to strengthen 'bourgeois democracy' while others regarded the Republic as the anteroom to socialism. Few, certainly, espoused revolutionary ideas in 1931; the party's immediate task, it was generally agreed, was to press for legislation aimed at assisting the working class and, in particular, the impoverished landless labourers of the south.

Spanish socialism was unique in Europe in 1931 in having to face serious anarchist competition for the allegiance of workers and poor peasants. The anarchist, or more accurately anarcho-syndicalist, CNT (National Confederation of Labour) had been founded in 1910–11; its main bastions were Catalonia, where socialist strength in the working class was virtually non-existent; Andalusia, where anarchism drew vigour from a long tradition of rural insurrectionism and millenarianism; Zaragoza; and parts of Asturias, Valencia and Galicia. Although chiefly associated in the public mind with acts of individual and collective violence, the CNT was a complex phenomenon. Broadly speaking, anarchists opposed political activity — parties, elections and parliaments — in favour of sustained trade-union struggle, faith in spontaneous revolution, and the idea of a revolutionary general strike. Rejecting all imposed authority and all forms of state, they embraced instead the vision of a post-revolutionary society that would be fully decentralized and truly self-regulating. Nevertheless in practice the CNT encompassed a wide variety of positions: dedicated anarchists both violent and pacific; trade-union reformists; and large numbers of workers who were trade-unionists first and anarchists very much second.

The CNT's response to the coming of a Republic was confused. Despite its official view that all states, republican as well as mon-archic, were equally repressive and repugnant, its members were at first by no means implacably hostile to a regime which promised

11

to inject an air of greater freedom into Spanish life. The possibility of the CNT's evolving in a more moderate direction, if not a strong one, certainly existed. However early clashes with the new authorities — desperate not to appear 'soft' on law and order — and the Socialist Party's clear determination to use its power to weaken its rival soon alienated the CNT from the Republic. Well before the end of 1931 radical elements within the organization had swept moderates aside and launched the CNT on a course of conflict with the Republic. CNT-inspired strikes between 1931 and 1933 frequently gave rise to clashes between workers and the two armed police forces, the Civil Guard and the Republic's new Assault Guard. Anarchist risings in January 1932, January 1933 and December 1933, while highly regionalized and easily suppressed, provided evidence of the Republic's failure to embrace a large part of the Spanish lower class and at the same time helped convince many middle-class Spaniards that Republican democracy was the breeding ground of disorder and revolution.

REGIONALISM

The politics of Spain's new democracy were greatly affected by her regional diversity. In all spheres of politics and legislation, regional variations — in, for example, landholding systems, types of economic activity, living standards and literacy levels — complicated the formulation and implementation of policy. Perhaps the thorniest problems of all were those created by the aspirations of regions whose linguistic and cultural identities were actually distinct from those of Spain, or more properly of Castile. The most immediately challenging case was that of Catalonia. This north-eastern region possessed a Romance language quite different from Spanish, a self-consciously 'European' culture, and — by Spanish standards — a 'modern', industrial economy. Since the mid-nineteenth century there had emerged in Catalonia a vigorous nationalist movement, most of whose protagonists nevertheless sought not separation from Spain but regional autonomy, the defence of Catalonia's distinctiveness and the enhancement of her position and influence within Spain as a whole. Through a wider acceptance of Catalonia's progressive outlook, 'Catalanists' insisted, all of Spain might be modernized.

By the 1930s the dominant force within Catalanism was the

Esquerra, a coalition of democratic and republican groups formed in 1930–1 under the leadership of Francesc Macià. The Esquerra possessed a powerful base of support within the region's urban lower-middle class and among the tenant vine-growers or *rabassaires*; through Macià's lieutenant and eventual successor, Lluis Companys, it also strove to maintain working relations with the CNT, whose members, despite their theoretical rejection of politics, sometimes provided it with their votes. The Catalan left's participation in the Pact of San Sebastian bound Spanish Republicans and Socialists, few of whom felt real sympathy towards the idea of regional autonomy, to a policy which was always certain to alienate the Spanish right.

Basque nationalism presented the Republic's leaders with different problems. Whilst Catalanism was at least acceptably 'progressive', Basque nationalism was seen by most Republicans and Socialists as 'reactionary'. The Basques, a people with a unique, non-Latin culture and, to the majority of Spaniards, an incomprehensible language, were for the most part devoutly Catholic and conservative. The Basque Nationalist Party (PNV) added to this general outlook a racial antagonism towards everything Spanish and an abomination of the social, economic and cultural changes affecting the Basque country in the early twentieth century. Large-scale industrialization and urbanization were bad enough as far as most Basque Nationalists were concerned; even worse was the descent upon their homeland of tens of thousands of 'Spanish' immigrant workers, many of whom were affiliated to the Socialist UGT. In 1931 it seemed unlikely that the Republic and the Basque Nationalists would ever be allies.

CATHOLICISM AND CONSERVATISM

During the Cortes debate on the draft constitution in the summer of 1931, Azaña declared that Spain had 'ceased to be Catholic'. Even if Catholicism had lost its grip on middle-class intellectuals like himself, and on the majority of urban and rural working-class Spaniards, Azaña's statement reflected a serious — and dangerous — misreading of the situation throughout much of provincial and particularly rural Spain, where religious devotion remained strong and the Church itself popular. Catholicism as an ideology and the Church as an institution were central to the strength of Spanish

13

conservatism both before and during the Republic, thanks to the power not only of school, pulpit and press, but also of a large and comprehensive network of church-sponsored social, professional and farmers' organizations within which much of the Catholic population was enmeshed.

Conservative Republicans like Maura and Alcalá Zamora, and even some individuals on the left, recognized the desirability of a *modus vivendi* between the Church and the Republic, and of the latter's attracting to it the Catholic sectors of the urban middle class and peasantry. Given the intensity of anticlericalism throughout so much of the Spanish left, however, the likelihood of this happening was never great. And although the Vatican was eager for peace with the new regime, powerful figures within both clergy and Catholic laity in Spain assumed from the start that conflict was inevitable and an aggressive posture towards the Republic accordingly required.

Catholic insecurity merged with the understandable fears of the wealthy, especially in the countryside, that the Republic would threaten landed property and in general favour the working class and peasantry over the employers and large landowners. With the disintegration of the parties of the old regime, conservatives who were unwilling to embrace the Republic wholeheartedly yet prepared to accept pragmatically the *fait accompli* of 14 April needed a new political organization. This quickly emerged in the shape of *Acción Nacional*, founded in late April 1931 as an 'electoral organization to bring together the elements of order'. The moving spirits of *Acción Nacional* were devout Catholics associated with the powerful lay organization Catholic Action and with the important Madrid newspaper *El Debate*, which on 14 April had advocated obedience to the *de facto* regime. Obedience did not imply approval, however. *Acción Nacional* propounded an 'accidentalist' attitude towards the Republic, involving a willingness to work within Republican democracy without accepting its permanence; regimes, accidentalists insisted, should be judged not by their form, monarchical or republican, but by their 'content'. Since the Republic's 'content' was almost certain to include anticlericalism and social radicalism, such statements were less flexible than they were calculated to sound.

Acción Nacional initially provided a temporary home not only for realists like the Salamanca lawyer José Maria Gil Robles, who in his memoirs (published thirty years later) was to admit to always

14

having been 'a monarchist at heart', but also for monarchist die-hards. As the months passed, however, the latter withdrew to pursue their goals separately. In April 1932 *Acción Nacional* was renamed *Acción Popular*; a year later this in turn became the core of a new mass Catholic-conservative party, the CEDA (Spanish Confederation of Autonomous Right-wing Groups). The CEDA, under Gil Robles' leadership, drew much of its strength from the network of Catholic organizations referred to earlier, most notably the CNCA (National Catholic-Agrarian Confederation). Its success — when founded it claimed over 700,000 members — reflected the failure of conservative Republicans to bring Spanish Catholics into the bosom of the Republic.

THE EXTREME RIGHT

The willingness of so many conservative Spaniards, rich and not so rich alike, to embrace 'accidentalism' condemned the extreme, openly anti-republican right to a state of deceptive weakness between 1931 and 1933. Nevertheless its three principal currents — Alfonsine monarchism, Carlism and undisguised fascism — were in the long run to play an important role in the destruction of Spanish democracy and the creation of the dictatorship that replaced it.

The oldest of the three by far was Carlism, a popular cause built around a dynastic dispute within the Spanish royal house of Borbón. By the 1930s Carlism had behind it a century's experience of political and military struggle against Spanish liberalism. Once widespread throughout much of northern Spain and embracing, among other things, rural and small-town resistance to centraliza-tion, capitalism and modernity, by 1931 it had shrunk in numbers and become an unambiguously reactionary movement of the Catholic right. The sudden arrival of the Republic, with its liberal and anticlerical atmosphere, probably saved Carlism from extinc-tion; certainly the cause now began to revive, expanding beyond its stronghold in Navarre into other regions, adopting a militantly anti-republican stance, and eventually developing a formidable paramilitary organization, the *Requeté*.

The Alfonsists, die-hard supporters of the exiled King, could command little popular support; they were, as one Carlist taunted them, a 'general staff without an army'. Their influence was never-theless far greater than numerical weakness might suggest, thanks

15

to their individual wealth and their connections with powerful financial, industrial and landowning interests. Through their press and journals, through such political organizations as *Renovación Española*, founded in early 1933, through their nurturing of Spanish fascism and subversion of the officer corps, the Alfonsists played an important part in undermining Spanish democracy and creating the ideological foundations of the Franco regime that emerged out of the Civil War.

While many Alfonsists became increasingly attracted to fascism after 1931, openly fascist organizations made little headway in Spain before 1936. The JONS (*Juntas de Ofensiva Nacional-Sindicalista*), founded late in 1931 by Ramiro Ledesma and Onésimo Redondo, and the Falange (Phalanx), founded in autumn 1933 by Primo de Rivera's son José Antonio, attracted little popular support before — or even after — their fusion in March 1934. Part of the reason may have been the 'foreignness' of their programmes; the Falange, despite occasional denials, followed Italian fascism in its exaltation of violence, desire for a totalitarian state, emphasis upon Spain's imperial heritage, and demagogic use of socially radical rhetoric to appeal to the working class. More important, however, was the fact that for the time being other parties of the right — the Carlists and especially the CEDA — commanded the support of those to whom fascism might otherwise have hoped to appeal. As 1936 was to prove, however, for very many Spaniards the choice of accidentalism over fascism was a matter of tactics rather than conviction.

Problems, policies and achievements

The Second Republic presented a serious challenge to the financial landholding and industrial oligarchy which still, in 1931, effectively controlled Spain. The challenge was only slightly weakened by the divergent preoccupations of middle-class Republicans and Socialists, the former stressing institutional reform and a transformation of social values and attitudes, the latter the redistribution of wealth, property and economic power. The problems facing a reforming democracy in Spain during the early 1930s were nevertheless enormous. In April—May 1931, when conservative forces were at their most vulnerable, the Provisional Government, conscious of lacking a clear mandate until a general election had

16

been held, shrank from attempting a 'revolution by decree'. Nor, at this stage, was there the slightest question of any social revolution from below; change, Republicans and Socialists agreed, should come democratically. Spain's dominant classes were therefore permitted the time and opportunity for marshalling their powerful opposition to the very measures that were intended to weaken them. Democratic reforms, certain to be costly, were rendered all the more difficult by the meagreness of the economic resources commanded by the Spanish state, given the ludicrously low level of direct taxation inherited from the monarchy, and by short-term problems arising from the world depression.

CHURCH, SCHOOL AND ARMY

The constitution of the Second Republic, passed in December 1931 after prolonged and sometimes heated parliamentary discussion, reflected the concerns of the Republican-Socialist alliance which, under Azaña's leadership, was to govern Spain until September 1933. While the affirmation that Spain was a 'Republic of workers of all classes' and clauses limiting absolute property rights bore a socialist ring, the prevailing tone was that of Left-republicanism. This was particularly true in the religious sphere. The constitution, after declaring that Spain no longer possessed an official religion, committed the Republic to recognizing freedom of worship, legalizing divorce, ending state support for the salaries of clergy, dissolving the Jesuit Order and nationalizing its property, and excluding other religious orders from participation in industry, commerce and education. These clauses unilaterally abrogated Spain's 1851 Concordat with Rome and, when carried into law during the next eighteen months, signalled an all-out legislative assault upon the Church's influential position within Spanish life. Outraged by the constitution's anticlericalism, the Catholic ministers in the Provisional Government, Alcalá Zamora and Maura, resigned in October 1931.

Relations between the Catholic Church and the new regime had begun to deteriorate even before the constitutional debate opened. Negotiations between the Republic and the Vatican languished; many Spanish bishops, including the primate, Cardinal-Archbishop Segura of Toledo, made little attempt to conceal their hostility to the Republic, Segura himself being eventually declared *persona non*

17

grata by the government; and in May 1931 Catholic sensibilities were outraged when the Provisional Government appeared unwilling to crush an outburst of church-burning and anticlerical violence in Madrid and several southern cities. The constitution guaranteed that church—state relations would remain difficult and that this in turn would imperil Spain's democratic experiment. To those activists of the Catholic right who eventually came together in the CEDA it was an illegitimate document calling for drastic 'revision'; more widely it helped to render the passive majority of Spanish Catholics immune from the appeal of conservative Republicanism and drive them into the CEDA's welcoming embrace.

Republicans were particularly concerned that the Church's educational role should cease and be superseded by a system of free, obligatory and laic education. In the sphere of educational reform the Republican—Socialist alliance moved swiftly. Some success was achieved in the primary field, where large numbers of new state schools were built and teachers trained. At secondary level, however, where replacement of the Church was more problematical, there is little doubt that the ban on church schools, where not flouted, was in the short term harmful to educational provision.

Apart from the Church, the institution whose role most perturbed Republicans was the army. Republicans like Azaña, Minister of War before — and after — he assumed the premiership in October 1931, wished to make the army militarily competent and politically neutral. Through a series of reforms, most notably the retiring on full pay of some 8,000 officers, Azaña went some way towards achieving the first of these goals. Political neutrality, without which a militarily improved army was liable to prove more of a threat than a support to Spanish democracy, was quite another matter. Admittedly the army had stood aside as the monarchy fell in April 1931, but its acceptance of the Republic was anything but unrestrained. Officers took unkindly to being reformed by a self-educated and self-appointed expert in civil—military relations; many, retired and active alike, began to conspire against a Republic which was increasingly seen to be not only anti-military but also 'soft' on the two issues that most obsessed military minds: regionalism and public order.

18

Despite the centralist tendencies of most non-Catalan Republicans and Socialists, the Republican—Socialist alliance could not escape its commitment to Catalan autonomy. The obligation arising from the Pact of San Sebastian was reinforced during the early days of the Republic, when the Esquerra leader, Macià, was only persuaded to withdraw his proclamation of a 'Catalan Republic within a Spanish Federal Republic' by the promise of early action on the autonomy issue and the immediate concession of a regional government, the *Generalitat* (Sp. *Generalidad*). This body, dominated by the Esquerra, proceeded to supervise the drafting of a Statute of Autonomy which was endorsed overwhelmingly by a plebiscite of the Catalonian population on 2 August 1931. The principle of regional autonomy having been legitimized in the Republican constitution, the Statute was finally approved by the Cortes in September 1932. Although in some areas the respective powers of the *Generalitat* and the Spanish state remained unclearly demarcated, with serious consequences in 1934, in general the Statute represented a balanced and satisfactory resolution of a complicated and sensitive issue. Its opponents, however, were unlikely to let the matter rest where it stood in September 1932. For while many Catalans may have felt that the Statute, especially in the financial sphere, went nowhere near far enough, the political right and much of the officer corps were incensed at what they considered the dismembering of the Spanish 'Fatherland'.

The Basques' progress towards autonomy was sluggish. Where the Esquerra's left-of-centre credentials made Catalan autonomy seem 'safe' to the Madrid government, the PNV's fervent Catholicism and general conservatism provoked Republican fears that an autonomous Basque region might become a base for right-wing subversion: what the Bilbao Socialist, Prieto, called a 'Vaticanist Gibraltar'. Republican suspicions were confirmed when the PNV, in pursuing autonomy, at first collaborated with the region's Carlists, the most inveterate enemies of Spanish liberalism. During the course of 1931—2, however, the Basque Nationalists yielded to pragmatism; appreciating that autonomy would only be possible if acceptable to those wielding power in Madrid, they effectively surrendered their more extreme goals, abandoned their right-wing allies, and moved closer to the Republicans and

Socialists. Even so, Basque autonomy was still a long way from being achieved when, during 1933, the left's grip on power started to loosen.

LAND REFORM

For the Socialists, the Republic's most important duty was to improve the lot of Spain's rural poor: a sincere commitment greatly reinforced by a radical change, dating from the late 1920s and climaxing in 1932–3, in the character of the UGT. Through an explosive expansion, especially in southern Spain, of its rural labourers' section, the FNTT (National Landworkers Federation), the UGT was suddenly transformed from an organization consisting primarily of skilled urban workers into one decisively influenced by the worst-off members of the agricultural labour force. The Socialist leadership's sensitivity to FNTT members' expectations meant that agrarian issues pressed even more urgently upon it than would otherwise have been the case.

Well before a bill to tackle the uneven distribution of land could go before the Cortes, Socialist ministers acted to alter the balance of power in rural Spain. Between April and July 1931 Largo Caballero at the Ministry of Labour and Fernando de los Ríos at the Justice ministry issued a series of decrees designed to protect the short-term position of tenant farmers and improve the wages, working conditions and bargaining position of rural labourers. The decrees, which later received parliamentary ratification, completely altered the social atmosphere in much of rural Spain and together represented the opening move in a challenge to the control of big landowners.

In September 1932, after several false starts and a tortuous parliamentary process in which the right, despite its numerical weakness, successfully employed filibustering tactics and hundreds of amendments in order to delay and dilute the original bill, an Agrarian Reform Act was finally passed. An Institute of Agrarian Reform was founded to break up large estates and redistribute them to landless labourers. Lacking adequate finance, information and technical expertise, and saddled with a piece of legislation riddled with loopholes and contradictions, the Institute was faced with an impossible task and had made little headway by the time the political climate changed in autumn 1933. FNTT members,

20

restrained by their leaders throughout 1932 despite the slowness of reform and the flagrant defiance by many landowners and rural employers of Largo Caballero's pro-labour measures, were by mid-1933 exhibiting signs of acute frustration and increasing militancy: attitudes shared, of course, by their anarchist counterparts in the CNT.

As well as failing to reward its rural working-class supporters, the Azaña coalition proved to have little to offer the large and politically pivotal class of small tenant farmers. Although a Rural Leases Bill designed to benefit tenants was placed before the Cortes, it was only half-heartedly pursued during 1932–3 and sank without trace when Azaña resigned from office in September 1933. The left's failure to woo with social legislation a class many of whose members it also alienated by its anticlericalism handed them on a plate to its right-wing opponents.

THE LIMITS OF DEMOCRATIZATION, 1931–3

The arrival of the Second Republic in 1931 undoubtedly created a new political and social atmosphere throughout most of Spain. Not only in large population centres but also in the countryside and small towns, those who had traditionally exercised power found themselves confronted, whether in newly constituted local councils or in the workplace, with a more open and popular style of politics and a more assertive lower class. As the dust created by the collapse of the monarchy cleared, however, it became increasingly apparent to those eager for change how tenacious and resourceful in defending their positions the established ruling classes of Spain were. In the political sphere, some embraced accidentalism and employed the social organizations of Catholicism in order to defend themselves. Others, more cynical, practised 'chameleonism' and declared themselves Republicans in the hope of taming the Republic; most of these attached themselves to the Radical Party, helping to turn it into, in effect, the conservative party of the Republic and increase its already considerable reputation for political and financial corruption. Either way, by 1933 it was evident how successful the holders of local socio-economic power had been in retaining it and in evading or openly flouting unwelcome legislation. Whilst under the protection of a sympathetic government the balance of power had unquestionably shifted perceptibly towards the lower classes,

21

landlords and employers remained sufficiently strong and confident to be poised for a counter-attack should the political climate change. With a Church and an officer corps also little weakened and increasingly hostile towards the Republic, the enemies of reform could be sure of powerful allies. The military revolt of General Sanjurjo on 10 August 1932 may have been premature and unsuccessful, but it was a significant straw in the wind.

If for the Spanish right the Republic had confirmed its promise as an uncongenial regime, for sections of the left it had by mid-1933 failed to fulfil hopes of far-reaching and irreversible social reform. Given the problems involved and the limited time available, such hopes were doubtless unrealistic; the fact remained that, in addition to the constant hostility of the CNT, Azaña and the Left–Republicans found themselves, by the summer of 1933, dealing with a Socialist Party gripped by frustration with parliamentary democracy. Impatience with the slowness of parliamentary and bureaucratic procedures, and a growing awareness that in the Spain of the 1930s the mere passage of social legislation did not guarantee its swift and successful implementation, were pushing leftwards not only the FNTT and other elements within the UGT, but also the Young Socialists, elements within the Socialist Party apparatus, and not least Largo Caballero himself. An end to unity on the left, and thereby of its political dominance, was in sight.

Polarization, 1933–6

The Azaña coalition reached its apogee in late 1932 with the defeat of Sanjurjo's rising and the passage of both the Agrarian Reform Act and the Catalan Statute. Thereafter its fortunes suffered a steep decline. The Casas Viejas incident of January 1933, involving a massacre of Andalusian villagers by government forces during an anarchist rising, provoked disgust on the left and a cynical outcry on the right, and began an eight-month process of governmental demoralization and disintegration. In April, a month after the 'moderate' right had come together in the ominously powerful and well-financed form of the CEDA, local elections provided encouragement both for the right and for a Radical Party now hungry for power. During the summer, the leftward drift of the Socialist Party quickened; although most Socialists continued to defend the Republic, faith in continued collaboration with non-Socialists was diminishing.

Azaña finally resigned in September 1933, following defeat for the government parties in elections for the Republic's supreme court. Interim power now passed to the Radicals, pending a general election. This was held on 17 November 1933, women voting for the first time. With the Socialists in most constituencies opting to go it alone in pursuit of an overall majority, the left was now divided. Unlike 1931, moreover, when many anarchists had cast votes in favour of Republican parties, the CNT adopted a policy of systematic abstention. The result was a shattering defeat for both elements of the Azaña coalition: Socialist strength was reduced to 58 seats and that of the entire Republican Left to 38, of which 22 represented Catalonia. In a triumph for the centre and right, the chief victors were the CEDA (117 seats) and the Radicals (104); some forty seats went to the extreme right of Carlists and Alfonsists. The Republic's ability to absorb the effects of dramatic electoral and governmental shifts was about to be tested.

DEMOCRACY ON THE DEFENSIVE, 1933—4

Although as the largest parliamentary party the CEDA might have expected to dominate government after the November 1933 election, this was ruled out by the President of the Republic, Alcalá Zamora, on grounds of the CEDA's non-republicanism. No doubt the President was, as his right-wing critics charged, jealous of the CEDA leader, Gil Robles, whose swift rise to prominence underlined his own failure to lead Spanish Catholics into the Republican camp. His suspicions of the CEDA were nevertheless genuine and, given its refusal to abandon accidentalism and wholeheartedly embrace the Republic, reasonable. Power therefore passed to the Radicals, who for the next two years dominated a series of coalition governments of increasingly right-wing complexion. CEDA support was essential throughout; in October 1934 three CEDA ministers finally entered the cabinet, and between May and September 1935 the number rose to five. On the Spanish left the period between the November 1933 election and the end of 1935 became known as the *bienio negro*, the 'two black years', during which the reforms of 1931—3 were reversed or flouted, socio-economic power reverted sharply to landlords and employers, the left itself experienced unprecedented repression and the seeds of civil war were decisively sown.

23

Historians have disagreed concerning how far the legislative record of the Radical-led but CEDA-manipulated administrations of these years should be regarded as deliberately undoing the work of 1931—3 in the religious, educational, regional, labour and agrarian spheres. To concentrate on new legislation or the statutory repealing of the old is, however, to miss the point. What really counted was the attitude of government to the implementation and observance of legislation, especially at local level, and here it is clear that from the moment the Radical leader, Lerroux, first assumed the premiership in September 1933 a dramatic reaction set in. During 1934 the advantage in rural Spain was allowed to swing violently back to landowners, landlords and employers, many of whom seized every opportunity to reverse by means of sackings, wage-cuts and evictions labour's modest gains of the previous two-and-a-half years.

Lerroux, believing that the pendulum had swung too far left in 1931—3, was now hoping to draw irreversibly into the Republican fold the conservative forces largely represented by the CEDA. Although if some sort of republic was to survive such a tactic made theoretical sense, its practicability was seriously undermined by the nature of the CEDA's ideology and wealthy support. Gil Robles had a 'tactic' of his own, involving a gradual advance towards 'full power' and a transformation of the Republic into what, it seemed likely, would be a 'corporate state' inspired by Catholic principles but also bearing some resemblance to Italian fascism. Quite apart from the fears this aroused on the left, the price of CEDA support was a return, especially in rural Spain, to the social situation of the monarchy — a course that could only have explosive consequences.

THE RESPONSE OF THE LEFT

The rank and file of both the Socialist movement and the CNT had been frustrated enough at the limitations of social reform under the Republic; when the Radicals and the right set about negating what little seemed to have been gained, militancy rose to new levels. The almost unanimous electoral abstention of CNT members in November 1933, in protest at the shortcomings of Republican reformism and the repressiveness of the Azaña governments towards the CNT itself, contributed significantly to the left's defeat. In December there followed the most extensive anarchist rising of the entire Republican period. Most serious in parts of Catalonia, in

Aragon and in neighbouring Rioja, the movement was eventually suppressed with military force; the strength and resilience of Aragonese anarchism were nevertheless still evident in the spring of 1934, when the regional capital, Zaragoza, was paralysed for weeks by a general strike.

Spanish socialism, meanwhile, was in the early stages of what was to be termed 'bolshevization': a shift towards revolutionary positions in which moderates like Prieto found themselves struggling to retain influence and party office. The Socialists' leftward lurch was stimulated not only by the accumulated frustrations of office but also by a fear of 'fascism', chiefly in the shape of the CEDA. Ideologically speaking the CEDA may not have been strictly fascist; however, in view of its authoritarian tendencies, the belligerent rhetoric of Gil Robles and other leading *cedistas*, the fascistic posturings of its youth movement, and the harshness of the social reaction it embodied, it is not difficult to understand the fears it aroused on the left. The crushing of the Austrian Socialists in February 1934 by a Catholic government ideologically close to the CEDA merely served to convince many Socialists, already acutely aware of the fate suffered by their Italian and German comrades, of the need to prepare for the worst. Largo Caballero, the anarchists' habitual enemy, now began to call for a 'Workers' Alliance' embracing the Socialists, the CNT, the small Spanish Communist Party and the rest of the working-class left.

As 1934 wore on, the atmosphere grew increasingly tense. The appointment of a hardline Radical, Salazar Alonso, to the Interior ministry in May signalled an even tougher governmental attitude on social issues and a desire to provoke desperate strikes in order to weaken labour and the left still further. In June the FNTT, under the pressure of rising rural unemployment and employer intransigence, called an agricultural labourers' strike, the swift collapse of which dealt a serious blow to the entire UGT. If this could happen with the CEDA merely exerting pressure upon the government from outside, the Socialist and Republican left wondered, what would the CEDA do if actually admitted to the cabinet? For the entire working-class left the answer seemed to be that the tragedy of Austria would be replayed in Spain; for the Republican left it was that the Republic would be constitutionally 'revised' out of existence. When, during the summer, disputes arose over the scope of Catalan autonomy and Basque local government, Catalanists and

25

Basque Nationalists concluded that the right was also bent upon reasserting central power.

In late September 1934, Gil Robles brought down the government and the CEDA was admitted to a reformed cabinet. The Socialist response was a general strike. In most of Spain, especially in the demoralized countryside, the strike quickly collapsed thanks to ill-preparedness, lack of resolution and determined government action. In the mining region of Asturias, however, it developed into a full-scale revolt involving not only UGT workers but also, in the first practical manifestation of the 'Workers' Alliance', the CNT and the Communists. A quite different rising occurred in Barcelona, where the Esquerra leader, Companys, was manoeuvred by extreme Catalan Nationalists into proclaiming Catalonia's independence. The Barcelona rising, which failed to enlist the vital support of the CNT, was quickly suppressed, but that in Asturias lasted a fortnight until finally crushed, with considerable bloodshed, by Spanish and Moorish troops commanded by General Francisco Franco.

FROM ASTURIAS TO THE POPULAR FRONT

After Asturias, the prospects for a democratic Republic were even bleaker than before. The most immediate consequence was the swingeing repression carried out during the autumn and winter of 1934—5. Mass arrests created over 30,000 political prisoners; much of the left-wing press, numerous left-controlled councils and the Catalan Autonomy Statute were suspended. The CNT — not for the first time under the Republic — was driven virtually underground and most of the UGT executive imprisoned. Even so the repression, thanks mainly to the moderating role of Lerroux and the Radicals, stopped short of the extremes urged by the monarchist right and much of the CEDA: judicial executions were few, while at least the left remained legal and the Catalan Statute in being. From the spring of 1935 the Republican left and the Socialists were therefore able to revive and eventually form a new alliance, the Popular Front, to resist 'fascism' in the future.

The left's recovery confirmed the opinion of many on the right in the months following Asturias that a precious opportunity to smash the left and destroy the Republic was being lost. Wiser heads, impressed by the scale and intensity of working-class militancy in a single region and recognizing that an ill-timed coup might merely provoke rather than prevent a nationwide revolution of the left, placed their faith in subtler tactics. It was probably Gil Robles' confidence that the right could achieve 'full power' electorally that restrained him, as Minister of War between May and December 1935, from using his position, and his carefully cultivated good relations with the army general staff, to engineer a military takeover. Another deterrent, undoubtedly, was his appreciation that, in the event of a successful coup, power was unlikely to revert to a civilian such as himself.

The CEDA-Radical partnership proved to have little positive to offer Spain in the wake of Asturias. Although Gil Robles and a sincere 'Social-Catholic' minority within the CEDA were anxious to demonstrate their reforming credentials, and thereby to retain the loyalty of their own peasant supporters, with a programme aimed at converting rural tenants into property-owners, they got nowhere in the face of opposition from monarchists and the reactionary majority of their own party. As for the Radicals, during 1935 the party began to break up under the strains of the relationship with the CEDA and a succession of financial scandals. When the third coalition government to include the CEDA fell in December 1935, Alcalá Zamora seized the opportunity to exclude the party from an interim cabinet pending a new election.

This was held on 16 February 1936 and for the first time in the history of the Second Republic involved an evenly matched contest between large, cohesive left- and right-wing alliances; the Radical Party virtually disappeared as a significant force, leaving the political centre effectively unrepresented. The confrontation was symbolic of the accelerating polarization which had occurred over the previous five years, with the Popular Front calling for a determined re-application of the policies of 1931—3 and the right for radical constitutional revision. The apocalyptic character of the two sides' respective visions of what the other's victory would mean offered graphic proof of their inability to coexist. For the Popular Front the right's victory would lead straight to 'fascism'; for the right, that of the Popular Front to 'Bolshevik' revolution.

THE OMINOUS SPRING OF 1936

The election of 16 February 1936 gave the Popular Front a narrow majority of votes but, thanks to the idiosyncrasies of the Republic's electoral system, a commanding parliamentary majority. Azaña promptly returned to power at the head of a purely Republican government, the Socialists preferring to shun cabinet responsibility. Having released thousands of political prisoners, the new government proceeded to re-introduce the educational, religious and agrarian policies of 1931—3; in addition autonomy was restored to Catalonia and promised to the Basque Nationalists, whose loyalty to the Republic was thereby secured.

It was nevertheless outside parliament and the cabinet room that Spain's future was being decided. Throughout much of the south, where since late-1935 chronic rural unemployment had been aggravated by climatic disasters, the rural poor celebrated the election victory with a new aggressiveness. Anticipating land reform, poor peasants and agricultural labourers occupied large estates in a number of southern provinces; several villagers, as in Yeste (Albacete), perished in the attempt at the hands of the Civil Guard. Although land-occupations and a rash of urban strikes were spontaneous and largely uncoordinated, rightists saw them as evidence of the revolution they had predicted would follow a Popular Front victory. With the CEDA's accidentalist tactic shattered by election defeat, the initiative on the right was passing to advocates of anti-Republican violence and conspiracy. The principal beneficiary of the CEDA's discomfiture was the fascist Falange. A barely significant political force throughout the two-and-a-half years since its foundation, the Falange now found its numbers swelling dramatically with disillusioned members of the CEDA Youth. In the streets of Madrid and other cities its blue-shirted militants stepped up anti-leftist terror in an attempt to de-stabilize the Republic.

Meanwhile, a serious conspiracy against the Republic was being hatched. The key plotters were senior army officers such as Generals Mola, Goded and Fanjul, together with middle-ranking officers hostile to another phase of Republican reformism and ideologically subverted since 1931 by right-wing propaganda. Although the titular head of the conspiracy was Sanjurjo, exiled to Portugal following his failed rising in 1932, it was Mola who in April assumed the role of 'Director'. Also drawn into the plot were the Carlists and other extreme right-wing political groups. The Carlists had been building up the paramilitary *Requeté* since the early days of the Republic and seriously preparing for a rising since 1934. When, in March

1936, Mola was appointed commander of the garrison at Pamplona, capital of the Carlist stronghold of Navarre, he established close contacts with the local Carlist leadership in the hope of enlisting the *Requeté* in the projected rising. The Alfonsists, now led by the tough and ambitious José Calvo Sotelo, helped things along with money and important contacts, as did leading *cedistas* including Gil Robles himself. Although the Falange was less central to the conspiracy, there was never any doubt that it would join in any right-wing rising that might occur.

In the face of widespread unrest, Falangist violence, rumours of conspiracies and the increasingly pugnacious demeanour of right-wing press and politicians, the Republic required from its leaders strength, unity and determination. These qualities largely failed to materialize. Although José Antonio Primo de Rivera and several other Falangist leaders were imprisoned and military commands half-heartedly reshuffled, neither the Falange's growth nor the military threat were significantly curbed. The only hope for firm government, willing to defend the Republic by confronting rightist subversion, vigorously prosecuting reform, yet allaying fears of social revolution, lay with Azaña, elevated to the Presidency of the Republic in May, and Prieto, the shrewd and combative leader of the Socialist Party's moderate wing. A Prieto premiership was nevertheless ruled out by a Socialist leadership within which Largo Caballero and the 'bolshevizers' were dominant. Unimpressed by Prieto's insistence that Socialist moderation was the best defence against an ever more apparent flight by conservative Spaniards towards fascism, Largo Caballero, flaunting the label of 'the Spanish Lenin' bestowed upon him by *Pravda*, preferred to beguile the Socialist rank and file with the prospect of an imminent collapse of capitalism and transition to socialism. As the Socialist left's relationship with the moderates in its own party deteriorated, so links with a suddenly expanding Communist Party grew closer. In March the youth movements of the two organizations fused, the Communist Youth in effect absorbing the Young Socialists in what was advertised as an act of left-wing fraternity. Whilst lacking serious revolutionary intentions or any clear revolutionary strategy, Largo Caballero and the Socialist left thus played their part in heating up the political atmosphere and making strong Republican government impossible.

Although the new Prime Minister, the sickly Galician Republican

Casares Quiroga, preferred to discount the existence of a serious conspiracy, and although the conspirators' preparations had not been easy, by the early summer all but the final pieces were in place for a military rising with strong right-wing civilian support. A blow against the Republic from the right was now merely a matter of time. When, on 13 July, Calvo Sotelo was assassinated by Republican police in retaliation for the killing of one of their number by a Falangist, the rebels had the perfect pretext for making their move.

3
The Civil War 1936–9

From rebellion to Civil War: July–November 1936

Whatever may have been in the minds of right-wing conspirators and left-wing militants during the 'ominous spring' of 1936, it was certainly not a prolonged civil war. The carefully worked-out plan of the military plotters was for as swift a takeover as possible; if, however, the ideal was a classic *pronunciamiento* along the lines of 1923, General Mola was not alone in appreciating that times had changed and that opposition would have to be overcome. The rebel officers' paramilitary allies, the Carlists and Falangists, were certainly eager to spill the blood of their left-wing enemies, yet they too thought in terms of days rather than years of actual military conflict. What turned the rising of 17–18 July 1936 into a civil war was, first of all, the rebels' failure, due to hesitation and division within the officer corps and the militarized police forces, to seize control quickly enough throughout the country; second, the decision of the Republican government to arm the UGT and CNT militias, which contributed to the defeat of the rising in important centres; and finally the intervention of foreign powers, enabling the two sides to continue the struggle indefinitely.

THE RISING AND THE RESPONSE

As planned, the military rising commenced in Spanish Morocco and the Canary Islands on 17 July 1936. In Morocco command was

31

assumed by General Franco, a late but important recruit to the conspiracy, flown there from the Canaries in a plane provided by British sympathizers. During 18—19 July the rebellion was taken up by garrisons on the Spanish mainland, spreading roughly northwards from Andalusia. It was quickly successful in those provincial capitals where garrison commanders were squarely behind the rebellion and where civilian sympathy was evident: for example in Pamplona, where thousands of Navarrese Carlists rushed to volunteer; in Burgos, the austere heart of Old Castile; and throughout much of conservative northern Spain. The rebels also succeeded, sometimes through audacity or sheer bluff, in a number of cities, such as the CNT stronghold of Zaragoza, Seville and Córdoba in Andalusia, and the Asturian capital of Oviedo, where the popular climate was distinctly less congenial. In other important cities, however, including Málaga in the south, Santander on the north coast, and the Basque city of Bilbao, the rising either failed to get started or was swiftly quelled by loyal troops and members of the two main armed police forces, the Civil Guard and Assault Guard. In several towns and cities, indeed, the attitude of the police proved decisive in tilting the issue one way or another.

With the rising far from achieving complete success, the outcome in Madrid and Barcelona was crucial. Amid an increasingly confused situation the central government in Madrid and the *Generalitat* in Barcelona found themselves facing demands that they distribute to UGT and CNT members arms with which to resist 'fascism'. Madrid saw three governments in a day. First Casares Quiroga, who had fatally underestimated the seriousness of what he called an 'absurd plot' and refused to arm the workers, panicked and made way for the more conservative Martínez Barrio. Having tried unsuccessfully to negotiate by telephone a compromise truce with Mola and other rebel commanders, he in turn resigned and was replaced by Azaña's friend José Giral. The difficult decision to arm the union militias was now taken, enabling workers to participate in crushing the rising in Madrid when, finally, it occurred. In Barcelona, when the president of the *Generalitat*, Companys, shrank from arming the CNT, the latter's members seized weapons from the arsenals; together with loyal police, they overcame the rebels and ensured the failure of the rising throughout Catalonia. Armed workers also helped tip the balance in the Basque city of San Sebastián and in Valencia, principal city of eastern Spain.

By 22 July, the date by which the military conspirators had hoped to be in control of the entire country, it was clear that the territory of Spain was split between the two camps (see map on p. xv). The rebels controlled a broad band of northern and north-western Spain, extending eastwards into Aragon but excluding most of the north coast; in addition they had triumphed in the Canaries, in Mallorca and Ibiza, in Spanish Morocco, and in pockets of Andalusia including four of its principal cities and the southernmost tip of the Spanish mainland between Cádiz and Algeciras. For the moment the Republic held most of the north coast, Catalonia, Minorca, and the greater part of southern Spain. This immediate stalemate could be ended in one of two ways: through a negotiated peace or a sudden change in the military circumstances of one or both sides. The former, following Mola's early rejection, was rendered even less likely by two unfolding developments: the Republican government's loss of authority throughout much of the area nominally under its control; and the bloodletting in both zones as zealots took revenge upon their political enemies. Only a military resolution of the situation was now possible, and it was difficult to see how this could come about quickly. Already, within a week of being launched, what the conspirators had intended as a smooth, swift, surgical *coup d'état* was turning into a full-scale civil war.

MILITARY AND ECONOMIC RESOURCES

In determining the outcome of *coups d'état* the decisive factors may well be preparation, timing, audacity and luck. The winning of civil wars, however, depends upon the distribution, mobilization and deployment of military, economic and, in the widest sense, human resources. An examination of the resources of the two sides at the start of the Spanish Civil War reveals how delicately these were balanced and underlines the influence that the manner of their use was likely to have upon the course of the conflict.

The role of loyal officers and police in the events of 17–20 July demonstrates that while the rising may have been predominantly military in character it was far from being a rising of *all* the military. In the event the army officer corps on the Spanish mainland divided roughly equally between rebels and loyalists: 75 per cent of divisional generals, 70 per cent of brigadier-generals and a majority of colonels stayed loyal, but lower-echelon and particularly younger officers sided overwhelmingly and enthusiastically with the rebellion. As of late July 1936 the rebellion could claim 62,000 officers and men, the government some 55,000. The balance within the militarized police forces tilted the other way: of some 68,000 Civil Guards and Assault Guards, 60 per cent remained loyal: surprisingly in view of the former's reputation as the hammer of the rural poor, but crucially for the early failure of the rising in many places. In the air force the government held a three-to-two advantage, while sailors' mutinies brought most of the navy over to the Republican side. These figures may be somewhat misleading, however; many of those army and police officers who remained 'loyal' undoubtedly did so more through geographical accident than conviction, and the Republic's leaders were inhibited from ever making full use of them.

Given the above balance of forces, what was to prove the decisive military element was to be found outside metropolitan Spain. The 24,000-strong Army of Africa, stationed in Morocco and commanded by General Franco, was incomparably the best fighting force in the Spanish army and one hundred per cent behind the rising. If — and given the Republic's apparent naval and air strength it was a big 'if' — the Army of Africa could be transported from Morocco to the mainland, the military advantage would shift dramatically towards the rebels.

In August 1936 Prieto claimed that the rebels were certain to fail owing to the Republic's superior economic resources. He certainly had a point. The government possessed the considerable gold and silver reserves of the Bank of Spain, while its territory contained Spain's chief industrial regions, notably the Basque coastal region with its iron, steel and armaments industry, and produced important export crops such as citrus fruits and olive oil. This apparent advantage over a predominantly rural rebel zone would only be maintained, however, if the Republic could hold on to its territory, overcome the isolation of the north coast from the rest of the zone, put its precious metal reserves to good use, pay for essential raw materials and feed its large urban population.

EARLY FOREIGN INVOLVEMENT

Although both sides in the Civil War were to make propaganda capital out of the international relationships of the other, neither was justified in suggesting that its enemy's pre-war foreign contacts had significant bearing upon the events of the Second Republic or the actual coming of the war. On the left, the attitude of Moscow and the Third International, in so far as they had any influence at all in Spain before the war, was to encourage Popular Front democracy and discourage revolution. On the right, while Italian and German agents were active in Spain and sympathetic to the Spanish right, they cannot be said to have exerted pressure upon it or materially to have assisted it in subverting the Republic. Although a monarchist deputation did visit Mussolini in March 1934 to solicit help in a possible future rising, little practical as distinct from rhetorical assistance was forthcoming.

Nevertheless by 19 July both sides were looking for foreign help. The Republican government was, of course, the legal government of Spain and as such entitled to expect to be able to purchase arms on the international market. The most obvious suppliers were the Republic's fellow democracies, Britain and France, especially the latter which in May had also elected a Popular Front government. On 19 July Giral accordingly requested arms and aircraft from the French Socialist premier, Léon Blum. As a result of Blum's initially sympathetic response, in early August modest quantities of French aircraft arrived in Spain. Well before the end of July, however, Blum was facing a cabinet divided on the issue, vociferous opposition from the French right, and clear signals from the Baldwin government in Britain that it would not welcome French support for the Republic. Blum therefore felt obliged to go back on his original commitment to aid Spanish democracy, and instead proposed that the main European powers agree on a policy of 'non-intervention' in Spain. By the end of August, non-intervention was officially a reality.

Blum's hope that non-intervention, if dutifully observed, would be in the Republic's interests made theoretical sense in the light of the already clear success of the rebels in attracting foreign help. During the first week of hostilities Franco made pleas for help to both Mussolini and Hitler. Mussolini was the more hesitant; having failed to respond to two telegrams from Franco requesting aid in the form of military or civilian aircraft, the Italian dictator eventually succumbed to the more flattering blandishments of the exiled Alfonso XIII and a high-level monarchist delegation. As a result, twelve Savoia-81 bombers, at a price of £1,000,000 cash-in-advance, left Italy for Spanish Morocco on 29 July; only nine arrived, the others having crashed en route. Hitler, approached by Franco on 22 July through two Nazi businessmen operating in Morocco, was from the outset more positive; identifying the rebels' chief short-term problem — their lack of the means to ferry the Army of Africa across to the Spanish mainland — he authorized the sending to Morocco of thirty Junker JU-52 transport planes. Between them the Italian and German aircraft made possible an air-ferry which during late July and early August bore the greater part of the Army of Africa across the Straits of Gibraltar to Seville. With the assertion of rebel air-supremacy in the area at the start of August, the process was completed by sea. The rising thereby received a new impetus — and, once begun, aid from Italy and Germany continued to arrive.

Meanwhile the Republic, effectively abandoned by its fellow democracies, had turned for help to the Soviet Union. The moment and circumstances were propitious. Since Hitler's accession to the German chancellorship in January 1933, Stalin had concluded that international fascism, which hitherto he had interpreted as the herald of capitalist collapse, posed a threat after all, not only to the left within European countries but also to the survival of the Soviet Union itself. His answer was the adoption during 1934—5 of a 'Popular Front' policy for resisting fascism; this involved Communist support for 'bourgeois democratic' governments threatened by fascism, together with Soviet efforts at courting the diplomatic friendship of the western European democracies. In responding to a plea for help from Spain's Popular Front government, Stalin was thus pursuing what he perceived to be the foreign policy interests of the Soviet Union. If, of course, the position of the hitherto weak Spanish Communist Party could be enhanced in the process, so much the better. What Soviet aid, the first consignments of which began to reach Spain in October 1936, was emphatically *not* intended to do was advance the cause of social revolution in Republican Spain.

THE ADVANCE ON MADRID

Between late July and early October 1936 the rebels drove home the advantage given them by Franco's agreements with Mussolini and Hitler. The military map of Spain at the start of the Civil War was a complex one, with both zones split into two: that of the rebels by a Republican-held strip in Extremadura, and that of the Republic owing to the isolation of the north coast. Several fronts therefore formed. In the north, while in Aragon the CNT militia pushed forward from Barcelona in an attempt to recapture the former anarchist stronghold of Zaragoza, elsewhere the rebels seized the initiative. From Pamplona the army and the Carlist *Requeté* advanced northwards and by September, with the help of Italian bombers, had seized Irún and San Sebastián, thereby cutting off the rest of the Basque country and the north coast from the French border. Other detachments headed south from northern, rebel-held cities in an advance on Madrid, only to find themselves humiliatingly held by urban militia groups in the Guadarrama mountains north of the city.

This last disappointment bestowed proportionately greater importance upon developments in the southern sector. While military, Falangist and Carlist units, fanning out from rebel-held Seville, Cádiz, Córdoba and Granada, set about conquering the rest of Andalusia, Franco's Army of Africa and its accompanying Moorish troops pushed rapidly northwards from their southern beach-head into Extremadura and towards Madrid. Resistance from left-wing militia forces and loyalist Civil and Assault Guards was intermittently intense but incapable of seriously holding up the advance. With the capture of Mérida on 10 August the two halves of Nationalist territory were united. The left-wing stronghold of Badajoz fell on 14 August and Talavera, the last significant town before Madrid, on 2 September.

The Nationalists' military advances were everywhere marked by the slaughter of leftist militiamen and of known left-wing and Republican activists. At least 2,000 died in Badajoz alone, most of them machine-gunned in the bullring; thousands more perished at the hands of the Legionaries, the Moors or the right-wing militias in other towns and villages of Andalusia and Extremadura. Nor was such repression restricted to the formerly conflict-ridden south, for even in less socially divided regions like Navarre and Mallorca, where actual military campaigning was non-existent, political executions numbered thousands. The terror was cold-blooded and deliberate, designed to eradicate all opposition, secure the Nationalist rearguard and instil fear into those who still awaited the rebel advance. There was to be no let-up: by the end of the Civil War at least 200,000 enemies of the Nationalist 'crusade' would have been executed in this way.

The two Spains

As it became evident that a full-scale civil war was in progress in Spain, foreign observers hastened to impose an imaginary order upon a confused reality by attaching neat labels to the two sides. According to taste and political outlook the one was 'Republican', 'Loyalist' or 'Red', the other 'Insurgent', 'Nationalist' or 'Fascist'. The truth was of course less simple. The Republican cause embraced — far from comfortably — conservative, Catholic Basque Nationalists; Catalanists of all complexions; moderate and left-wing Republicans; right- and left-wing Socialists; Stalinist and anti-Stalinist Communists; and anarchists. With each group possessing its own goals, vision of the war's purpose and views as to how it should be fought, 'Republican' unity during the early months of the war was agonizingly difficult to achieve.

The forces of Nationalist Spain represented a coalition too: of military insurgents, Falangists, Carlists, Alfonsist monarchists, CEDA supporters, and assorted independent conservatives, Catholics and opportunists. Consciousness of this fact, plus a desire to court moderate Republican opinion, ensured that early rebel pronouncements were limited to vague calls for the prevention of left-wing revolution, the maintenance of national unity and the restoration of authority; beyond that it remained unclear whether the rising, if successful, would produce a conservative, more authoritarian republic, a monarchist restoration, a military dictatorship or perhaps even an out-and-out fascist state.

During the first year of the Civil War the issues of unity and authority were largely resolved in both zones. For the Republic the experience was a painful and, some would always argue, self-defeating one; for the Nationalists, united by a common deference towards authority, matters proceeded more smoothly — and in such a way as to determine Spain's future for almost forty years to come.

REVOLUTION AND AUTHORITY IN REPUBLICAN SPAIN

In the aftermath of the July rising the Republic faced the threat not only of military overthrow but also of its own disintegration. Across much of Republican Spain, established authority collapsed as often suspect local councils and police were swept aside by armed villagers and trade unionists. Grassroots power now passed to 'anti-fascist' committees, variously constituted according to the local balance of left-wing allegiance. At regional level, too, new sources of authority emerged; in the coastal Basque provinces, cut off from the heartland of Republican Spain, the separate Basque Republic of Euskadi came into existence; in Catalonia, where Companys reached an accommodation with the CNT, an anti-fascist Militia Committee ran affairs independently of Madrid; and in October Aragon became an autonomous CNT fief administered by its own regional 'Council'. For the next year the Republican government was obliged to struggle to reassert its authority.

In some instances, new organs of authority represented merely an extemporized response to the sudden appearance of a power vacuum. Elsewhere they were associated with a spontaneous and far-reaching social revolution in which the moving spirits were the CNT, the left wing of the UGT and, in Catalonia, the POUM — a small but vigorous anti-Stalinist communist party. Throughout wide areas, land, industry, commerce and services underwent collectivization. The process was very uneven. Madrid and Valencia continued to present a relatively conventional face to the world, while in PNV-dominated Euskadi no collectivization whatsoever occurred. In Catalonia, Aragon and Republican-held Andalusia, however, a new revolutionary order appeared in the process of creation, enthusiastically supported by the urban and rural working class if not always by the lower-middle class and landholding peasantry. The military arm of the revolution was the workers' militias, believed by their advocates to be both necessary to defend the revolution and capable of defeating fascism through their members' commitment to the new society.

In many areas the revolution was accompanied by the summary execution of the local ruling class — landowners, *caciques*, police and priests. The toll was considerable — as many as 6,000 priests, for example, may have died within Republican Spain — and a stain upon the Republic's reputation. Nevertheless it must be recognized that most of the killing of rightists in the Republican zone was spontaneous and that the government sought, successfully in the long run, to bring it to an end. The contrast with the deliberate and sustained pursuit of leftists in the Nationalist zone needs no further elaboration.

The dispersal of power and the divisive potential of the revolution created grave problems for a Republican government threatened by the Nationalists' advance on Madrid. The Giral government, consisting entirely as it did of bourgeois Republicans, was increasingly irrelevant to the new situation. On 4 September 1936 it was therefore replaced by a genuine 'Popular Front' government, headed by Largo Caballero and containing Socialists and Communists. For all his shortcomings Largo Caballero was the only political figure with sufficient standing on the left to have any chance of harnessing the revolution to the cause of victory; his advocacy of 'Workers' Alliance' between 1934 and 1936 had helped to dissipate some of the mutual antagonism which had previously soured his relations with the CNT, while his role as the 'Spanish Lenin' during 1936 had made possible a close relationship with the Spanish Communist Party. These links were crucial, given the numerical strength and revolutionary role of the CNT and the leverage available to the Communists once Soviet aid began to arrive in October. On 4 November, in one of the twentieth century's most ideologically self-sacrificial gestures, members of the CNT swallowed their hostility towards the exercise of authority and joined the Republican government. Two days later, with the Nationalists on the western outskirts of Madrid, the government left the beleaguered and, it was unanimously believed, doomed Spanish capital for the safer haven of Valencia.

THE COMMUNISTS AND THE REPUBLIC

The breadth of Largo Caballero's government in no sense reflected unanimity among its members concerning the nature and imperatives of the war. Two schools of thought emerged during the summer of 1936. For the anarchists, the POUM and sections of the Socialist left the social revolution within the Republican zone had become the chief reason for fighting fascism and, indeed, the only basis upon which workers and poor peasants could be expected to fight it. Bourgeois Republicans and right-wing Socialists like Prieto, Minister of Navy and Air in the Largo Caballero cabinet, and Dr Juan Negrín, Minister of Finance, argued that collectivization caused economic disruption and would alienate the lower-middle class and better-off peasantry from the Republic. As for the militias, however zealous and heroic, they had no chance of triumphing over the Nationalist armies. Governmental authority must be restored, the economy and war-effort be efficiently managed, and the chaotic militias be replaced by a disciplined conventional army.

These anti-revolutionary views coincided with those of the Spanish Communist Party, dutifully following Stalin's 'Popular Front' line of solidarity with bourgeois democrats in the anti-fascist struggle. Revolution in Spain, the Communists insisted, must be postponed until victory had been won and the appropriate 'objective conditions' had developed. As Soviet aid, Communist-sponsored volunteers, and Comintern agents entered Spain during the winter of 1936—7, Communist influence increased both inside and outside the government. So did membership of the Spanish Communist Party, its social conservatism and emphasis upon discipline appealing to many professional people, army officers and members of the urban and rural lower-middle classes.

By the spring of 1937 the Largo Caballero government had gone some way towards taming the process of social revolution and absorbing the militias into a regular army built around the Communists' own Fifth Regiment. The social revolution had not, however, been completely reversed. Largo Caballero was unwilling to move as far or as fast in an anti-revolutionary direction as his Communist, Republican and moderate Socialist colleagues wished. Moreover, he was becoming increasingly annoyed at the Communists' blatant attempts to maximize their influence wherever it mattered — in, for example, the army and the administration — and to dictate strategy. For their part, the Communists, and even more their Soviet and Comintern masters, were becoming impatient with the Premier's uncooperativeness and low credibility as a war leader. With antagonism growing between the Communists and their CNT and POUM rivals, the politics of Republican Spain were about to enter a new phase.

Crisis erupted in early May 1937 in Barcelona, in the shape of the 'civil war within the Civil War' so graphically described by George Orwell. Four days of street-fighting between the CNT and POUM on one side, and the Catalonian Communists of the PSUC (Unified Socialist Party of Catalonia) on the other, ended with the Communists victorious and Barcelona occupied by troops of the

Valencia government. When Largo Caballero resisted Communist pressure to dissolve the POUM and arrest its leaders, the Communists decided that the time had come to get rid of him. On 16 May 1937 they contrived a cabinet crisis; Largo Caballero resigned as premier and was replaced by Negrín, at the head of a cabinet free of left-wing Socialists and which the anarchists chose not to join. The clear policy of the Negrín government was the pragmatic pursuit of victory, involving the reversal of the revolution, assertion of governmental authority and the Republic's democratic credentials, and maintenance of good relations with the Soviet Union. During the late spring and summer of 1937 the revolution was well and truly rolled back in two of its former strongholds: Catalonia, which ceased to be autonomous within Republican Spain, and Aragon, where the CNT-dominated Council of Aragon was physically destroyed by Communist forces. The POUM became the object of a ruthless and bloody purge, and its leader, Andreu Nin, was captured, tortured and killed by the Soviet secret police. Although the strong-minded Negrín was never the Communist catspaw his many critics accused him of being, there was little he could do in the circumstances to prevent the Communists from exercising an increasingly independent and even dominant role within Republican Spain.

Nationalist Spain: The rise and rise of Francisco Franco

At the start of the 1936 rising, Francisco Franco was certainly not marked out as its eventual *generalísimo*, much less as the future leader of Spain. His military capacities, demonstrated in Morocco during the 1920s, were well known and respected, and his importance to the conspiracy as the designated commander of the Army of Africa was central. Nevertheless other generals — Sanjurjo, the nominal head of the rebellion; Mola, its 'Director'; or the arch-conspirator Goded, who was named to lead the rising in Catalonia — appeared more likely overall leaders. Quite apart from Franco's youth — he was only 44 in 1936 — his cautiousness towards involvement in conspiratorial activity had attracted criticism from many fellow officers, some of whom scornfully dubbed him 'Miss Canary Islands of 1936'. When the rebels formed a provisional National Defence Junta a week after the start of the rising, Franco was not a member, although he became one a few weeks later.

Franco's rise to military and political supremacy within Nationalist Spain was nevertheless meteoric. Sympathizers saw in this the hand of providence, while enemies suspected 'dirty tricks'. Luck and favourable circumstances certainly played an important part. Sanjurjo perished at the very outset when the plane taking him back to Spain from his Portuguese exile crashed on take-off. Goded was imprisoned when the Barcelona rising collapsed, and later executed. Mola found himself commanding difficult campaigns in northern Spain and was damaged by the Carlist connections about which he himself felt uneasy. As for possible civilian contenders for political leadership, Calvo Sotelo was dead before the war began, Gil Robles remained discredited by political failure, and José Antonio was languishing in a Republican jail.

While the removal of individual rivals unquestionably smoothed Franco's path to power, what really launched him upon it was the role allotted to him in the rising and the manner in which this role was played out. Command of the Army of Africa placed him in a decisive position once the initial impetus of the rising in peninsular Spain was lost. His successful dealings with Mussolini and Hitler, necessary in order to get his forces across the Straits of Gibraltar to Spain, ensured him a relationship with the Nationalists' powerful allies such as no other rebel commander came close to possessing. The dynamic campaign then waged under his command during the late summer of 1936 drew him into the spotlight as Nationalist Spain's most successful general. When, in late September 1936, the National Defence Junta, having recognized the need for an overall military commander, met in Salamanca to choose one, there was already only one serious candidate. On 28 September Franco accepted the positions of *Generalísimo* of the armed forces and 'Head of the Government of the Spanish State' with 'all the powers of the New State'. This assumption of political power as well as military command represented little short of a coup by Franco and a group of military and civilian supporters, mostly of monarchist sympathies; within days Franco had quietly promoted himself to 'Head of State', a title he was to retain until his death 39 years later.

THE FORGING OF THE FRANCO DICTATORSHIP

The issue of Nationalist Spain's overall leadership may now have been settled but the precise shape of the emergent new state had not. For Franco, the most problematical feature within the Nationalist zone was the continued existence of independent and competing political movements. By far the most important, by virtue of their numbers, were Carlism and the Falange, both of which had expanded considerably — in the Falange's case enormously — since the start of the war. The Carlists mainly recruited conservative Catholics suspicious of Falangist fascism; the Falange, in common with other European fascist movements in their periods of explosive growth, absorbed tens of thousands of new members from all quarters of the political spectrum, from ex-*cedistas* to Republicans and even leftists anxious to combine self-preservation with a semblance of socio-political 'radicalism'.

In the months following his elevation, three considerations pushed Franco towards drastically altering this situation. In the first place, of course, the survival of autonomous and independently-minded political movements threatened his personal authority and could, in the long run, undermine his very position as Head of State. Even if the Carlists were unlikely ever to possess more than nuisance value, the Falange, with its wider appeal and rapid growth-rate, was a different matter. The second reason was more disinterested: a simple unwillingness to tolerate during wartime political divisions which might — as in the Republican zone — lessen military effectiveness. Thirdly, Franco and advisers such as his brother-in-law, Ramón Serrano Suñer, looking ahead to a post-war Spain and impressed by Italian and German precedents, were becoming increasingly attracted to the idea of a single-party and perhaps even totalitarian state.

During the winter of 1936—7, Franco therefore brought the right-wing militias firmly under army control and set about establishing his authority over the political parties themselves. In this he was undoubtedly assisted by problems within both mass parties. In the Falange's case the principal issue was leadership; when José Antonio Primo de Rivera, jailed in Alicante since before the start of the war, was executed in November 1936, he left behind him a movement riddled with factionalism and cursed with second-rate would-be successors. Carlism, too, was plagued by internal divisions and offered no resistance when, in December 1936, Franco effectively exiled its political leader, Fal Conde, for too strenuously asserting his movement's independence. The day of reckoning came on 19 April 1937, when Franco issued the Decree of Unification, creating the single party of Nationalist Spain. Within the grotesquely labelled *Falange Española Tradicionalista y de las JONS*, to be more manageably known as the FET or National Movement, under his own leadership Franco combined the Falange, the Carlists and the other, smaller political factions of Nationalist Spain. In the event, this ambitious and seemingly provocative move took effect with remarkable ease. Although many Carlists and Falangists naturally disliked the Unification, with their fighting men busy at the front there was little they could do to resist it, especially since they shared the general Nationalist respect for 'authority'. In any case, many others within both parties were amenable to the new order and rushed to grab jobs in the FET apparatus.

The 'Unification' of April 1937, and the appointment in January 1938 of the first Nationalist cabinet, proved to be the first steps in the creation of the authoritarian regime which, following the Nationalist victory in 1939, was to govern Spain for another 36 years. Within this regime, as it already existed by the end of the Civil War, the salient features were the prominent, but in no sense governing role of the FET; the restoration of the Catholic Church to a position of monopoly in education and of powerful cultural influence; the ruthless repression of all forms of opposition; and above all, the unassailable position and total dominance of Franco himself.

The military struggle

THE REPUBLIC IN RETREAT: NOVEMBER 1936 – JANUARY 1938

Contrary to universal expectation, Madrid did not fall in November 1936. It might perhaps have done so had Franco not delayed his assault in order to make a detour eastwards to Toledo. The relief of the town's Alcázar, the military barracks where the Nationalist garrison was under siege from left-wing militias, while earning Franco the world's headlines and assisting his elevation to overall military and political command, also gave the Republicans precious time in which to organize the defence of the capital. When the attack finally came Madrid withstood it, thanks in part to the courage of the left-wing militias and the ordinary people of the city, and in part to the stiffening effect of the first International Brigades

— foreign volunteers organized by the Comintern, who arrived at the crucial moment. For several more months Madrid remained the focus of the fighting, as the Nationalists sought to surround the city and the Republicans to cut their enemy's lines of communication. However, while battles such as those of the Jarama (February 1937), Guadalajara (March 1937) and Brunete (July 1937) were fought bitterly and with heavy casualties on both sides, as the Civil War entered its second year the fronts around Madrid had changed little since the previous November.

Elsewhere, the war was more mobile. In February 1937 the southern coastal city of Málaga was taken by Spanish and Italian forces, and its capture was followed by another massacre of leftists. Between April and September 1937 the rest of the isolated north coast — the Basque province of Vizcaya, Santander and Asturias — fell to the Nationalists. This brought to an end the short life of the Basque Republic of Euskadi, which under its president, Aguirre, had been waging what was very much its own war. The fall of Vizcaya was preceded by one of the Spanish Civil War's most notorious actions: the bombing of the Basques' spiritual capital, Guernica, by the German Condor Legion, acting on the instructions of the Nationalist High Command. The conquest of the north decisively tilted the scales in Franco's favour; quite apart from the damage to Republican morale, it brought the Nationalists raw materials — iron ore and coal — and industrial capacity vital to the prosecution of modern warfare.

The course of the war between the Madrid stalemate and the beginning of 1938 clearly illustrates some of the two sides' military strengths and weaknesses. In terms of military organization the Republic made considerable progress between the chaotic summer of 1936 and the second half of 1937. The disciplined regular army desired by Prieto and, of course, by the Communists was brought into being, and in the process competent commanders were discovered: men like Vicente Rojo, chief-of-staff from November 1936; Miaja, the 'saviour of Madrid'; the Communists Modesto, Lister and Valentín González 'El Campesino'; and the anarchist Cipriano Mera. Nevertheless the Republicans, plagued by continuing factional disputes over strategy, tactics and supply, proved unable to recapture lost territory. Republican offensives at Brunete, west of Madrid (July 1937), Belchite in Aragon (August—September 1937) and further south in Aragon at Teruel (December 1937—

February 1938) followed a similar pattern whereby small but costly gains of territory were quickly followed by its still more costly surrender to the counterattacking Nationalists. The latter, meanwhile, settled in and around Madrid and concentrated upon advances elsewhere. In Franco they possessed a leader who, notwithstanding German and Italian annoyance at his lack of dynamism and broad vision, was a first-rate field commander, devoted to the gradual but irreversible conquest of territory and with it the total subjection of the Spanish population.

During the course of 1937 the impact of foreign involvement — and non-involvement — upon the war became both more apparent and more complex. Let us now, therefore, examine more closely this aspect of the Spanish Civil War.

FOREIGN INTERVENTION AND NON-INTERVENTION

The course of the Spanish Civil War was crucially affected by the Anglo-French adoption of, and adherence to, the policy of non-intervention, and the similar determination of US President Roosevelt to observe the strictest neutrality towards the Spanish struggle. Not that there was ever any question of the western democracies intervening *directly* in the fighting; what was at stake was the right of the Republic's legally elected government to purchase arms, ammunition and military supplies from its fellow democracies. The French, British and United States governments were swayed in their unwillingness to recognize this right by rather different considerations. In France, bitter political divisions, fear of foreign military entanglement and deference towards Britain forced Blum and the Popular Front government to reverse their initial policy of assisting the Republic and instead embrace non-intervention in the sincere hope of persuading other powers to keep out of Spain too. The maintenance of this posture was ensured by the generally rightward shift of French cabinets between 1936 and 1939, interrupted only by Blum's shortlived second government in early 1938 when aid was briefly resumed.

For their part, the Conservative-dominated National governments of Baldwin and Chamberlain in Britain, engaged in their policies of appeasement towards the fascist powers, were anxious to prevent the Spanish war from spreading, even at the cost of turning a blind eye to the involvement of Italy, Germany and the Soviet

Union. Moreover, within the Conservative Party, while some mavericks — like, albeit belatedly, Churchill — recognized that peace in Europe would be best served by the defeat of fascism in Spain, hostility towards the Spanish 'Reds' and sympathy for Franco predominated: views shared in the business community, many of whose members continued to trade with Nationalist Spain throughout the war. Labour and Liberal devotion to the Republican cause, while strong and passionate, was incapable of deflecting the course of British policy. In the United States, fear of European embroilment and the pro-Nationalist zeal of many American Catholics effectively cancelled out the sympathy felt in liberal circles towards the Republic.

The institutional manifestation of non-intervention was the Non-Intervention Committee, set up in London in September 1936 to supervise the application of a principle observed by the democracies and by smaller European countries but openly flouted by Europe's three most powerful dictatorships. The Soviet, Italian and German governments naturally justified their own infringe-ment of non-intervention, to which they officially subscribed, by reference to the conduct of the other side. Eden, the British foreign secretary, declared that non-intervention, 'a leaky dam, but better than no dam at all', prevented the outbreak of a general war. No-one can say for certain whether he was right; what can be stated with certainty is that with Italy and Germany helping the Nationalists almost from the beginning, non-intervention threw the Spanish Republic into the embrace of the only great power will-ing to help her — the Soviet Union.

For two years following October 1936, Soviet aid helped the Republic to fight on. The aid itself took various forms: arms and ammunition, including perhaps 1,000 aircraft and 700 tanks; Soviet and Comintern military — and political — advisers; and the Inter-national Brigades: a total of nearly 60,000 foreign volunteers from all corners of the world, many of them refugees from fascist regimes or veterans of anti-fascist struggles, recruited and trained in the main by Communists. The price paid by the Republic for this help was high. As financial payment the Government had no alternative but to permit the dispatch of most of its gold and silver reserves to the Soviet Union. Of far more significance to the war itself, however, was the political price represented by acceptance of Communist leverage within Republican Spain, and all that this proved to carry with it: interference in the composition of cabinets and the formulation of strategy; the reversal of social revolution; the persecution of political enemies; and the steadily declining popular morale. Soviet aid was never intended in any case to equip the Republic for victory, so much as to enable it to resist until the Spanish war became part of a more general conflict in which Britain and France would join the Soviet Union in fighting European fascism. Once the Munich Agreement of October 1938 appeared to dash any such prospect, Stalin lost interest in Spain and help for the by then desperate Republic dried up. The Soviet Union proved an unreliable friend.

The Nationalists fared better in their foreign dealings. In terms of sheer quantity the material and human help provided by Mussolini and Hitler — aircraft, tanks, armoured vehicles, small arms and ammunition, the 70-80,000 Italian 'volunteers' and the German Condor Legion with its own 600 aircraft and 200 tanks — may or may not have exceeded Soviet aid to the Republic. More important was that German and Italian aid tended to arrive on request, and especially when most needed following Nationalist setbacks or preceding major pushes; that it was channelled through Franco as Nationalist leader and not, as with Soviet aid to the Republic, through a political faction; and that it came on easy credit terms with no political strings attached. Although the Germans sought with some short-term success to turn Nationalist Spain into an economic dependency, neither they nor the Italians interfered significantly in the internal politics of Nationalist Spain.

THE DEATH AGONY OF THE REPUBLIC, JANUARY 1938–MARCH 1939

Non-intervention and the differential impact of foreign aid upon the two sides made a Republican victory all but impossible. What is remarkable is that Republican resistance continued for so long after the loss of the north in mid-1937 — a tribute to improved military organization and human courage. Another factor was the legendary cautiousness of Franco, for whom slow progress and sure gains were always to be preferred to unnecessary risks. However slowly, the Nationalists' gradual conquest of Spain continued. In April 1938 their eastward advance reached the Mediterranean near Castellón, cutting Catalonia off from the rest of Republican Spain. Had the advance been sustained, perhaps Catalonia would have fallen quickly; instead Franco — possibly, in the tense international atmosphere of mid-1938, fearing actual French intervention were he to approach the French frontier — turned south towards Valencia, only to find his offensive halted by Republican resistance. In July there commenced the final Republican offensive of the war: the crossing of the river Ebro by 80,000 men in an attempt to reunite Catalonia with the 'central zone'. If the siege of Madrid was the first major epic of the Civil War, the Battle of the Ebro, similarly recorded in song, poetry and prose, was the last. The battle lasted for over three months, repeating on a massive scale the established pattern of Republican offensives: an early breakthrough followed by retreat and heavy losses — on this occasion 20,000 Republican fatalities and 55,000 wounded or captured. After the Ebro, Catalonia could not be expected to hold on for long, and if Catalonia fell the rest of Republican Spain was likely to follow.

It was the unhappy fate of Juan Negrín to be Prime Minister of the Spanish Republic throughout its protracted agony. If Largo Caballero's task had been difficult, Negrín's was impossible. The Republic's continued dependence upon the Soviet Union guaranteed the Communists an influence within Republican Spain that the pragmatic premier could do little to resist. The achievements of the Communists and their Comintern helpers in the purely military sphere, as exemplified by their contribution to the formation of the Republican Popular Army, were considerable; if they created little likelihood of a Republican victory, certainly they postponed its defeat. The Communists' negative achievement was the souring of the political atmosphere of Republican Spain. Through their attack upon the social revolution, their politicization of the armed forces, their intolerance of opposition, and, most of all, their extensive use of brutal secret police methods via the SIM (Military Investigation Service), they helped to convince many inhabitants of the Republican zone that fascist oppression could be little worse than that under which they were already living.

During 1938 war-weariness and pessimism began seriously to affect Republican Spain. Malnutrition was now added to other reasons for demoralization as Republican territory and agricultural resources contracted. To a population existing on 'Dr Negrín's Resistance Pills' — lentils — leaflets dropped from Nationalist aircraft, informing them of the plentiful food in the Nationalist zone, were weapons as potent as bombs. The information was also accurate; Nationalist Spain, based on the agricultural regions of Spain and constantly expanding its territory faster than its population, was never short of food. Among the leading figures of Republican Spain to conclude that sooner or later defeat was unavoidable were the President, Azaña, and Prieto; in April 1938 the latter, following a Communist-orchestrated campaign, was ejected from his post as Defence Minister on grounds of 'defeatism'. Hopes of a compromise peace stood no chance in the face of Franco's determination to pursue the Republic's unconditional surrender. Negrín was obliged to go on hoping that the outbreak of a general war would at last bring the democracies to the Republic's aid: a vain enough hope following the Anglo-Italian Naval Treaty of April 1938 but an even vainer one, as Stalin realized, after Munich. The British and French recognition of the Franco regime in late February 1939 merely underlined the hopelessness of the Republic's diplomatic position.

After two-and-a-half years of stubborn resistance, the Republic collapsed rapidly during the first three months of 1939. Catalonia fell to the Nationalists during January and early February; as Franco's armies advanced, taking 200,000 prisoners, half a million civilian and military refugees fled before them into France, among them Azaña and several members of the Republican government. The 'central zone' went the same way during March, its collapse preceded by a second 'civil war within the Civil War': a tragicomic affair in which 'rebels' under Colonel Casado, anxious to negotiate a surrender, engineered a coup and then clashed with Communists eager to fight to the last. In Madrid Casado triumphed and at the last moment Communist power was broken. It was to no purpose, however, for Franco was no more inclined to negotiate now than at any time in the past year. On 26 March the Nationalists entered Madrid, by the end of the month they had occupied the rest of the Republican zone and on 1 April Franco declared the Civil War at an end. As right-wing supporters, many appearing in public for the first time in almost three years, welcomed their liberators with monarchist flags and fascist salutes, many other Spaniards faced a terrifying future: so terrifying, indeed, that to some suicide was preferable. Several hundred thousand Spaniards and non-Spaniards had died on the battlefields of Spain between 1936 and 1939; at least 200,000 more were to be executed during the next few years, 2,000,000 would suffer imprisonment or forced labour, and millions more again faced a lifetime of discrimination for having fought on behalf of the Republic. In a purely military sense the Spanish Civil War may have ended on 1 April 1939, but for its victor, Francisco Franco, it would never truly end.

4

Interpretations, debates and conclusions

Having aroused such passions in its day, the Spanish Civil War has inevitably inspired disagreement among historians. For many years the Franco regime saw to it that within Spain itself only pro-Nationalist accounts of the 1930s could be published, leaving the field of serious scholarship to foreigners, mostly from Britain and the United States. Even they found access to many important historical sources difficult or impossible. With the coming of a new democracy to Spain, however, the situation has been transformed; enormous quantities of previously inaccessible research materials have become available to historians, and now, quite properly, it is the Spaniards themselves who are at the forefront of research, publication and the challenging of old orthodoxies. Debate concerning the Spanish Civil War and its origins therefore remains vigorous. The sections that follow represent an attempt to examine briefly some of the liveliest areas of debate.

Why did Spanish democracy fail?

Since historians are creatures of flesh and blood, often with passionate convictions and opinions, and since the Spanish Civil War represents a recent historical event of unusual political, ideological and emotional content, it is hardly surprising that historical accounts of the 1931—6 period often appear to lack the objectivity attainable to students of episodes further in the past. Few historians, admittedly, have sought to criticize the *attempt* to democratize a country so clearly and grossly racked by inequality, though most have quite reasonably stressed the unavoidable difficulties that such an attempt posed. Disagreement has tended to centre upon the issue of responsibility for the evident political incompatibility of left and right and the consequent unworkability of Republican democracy. Individual attributions of guilt point to left or right often according to the ideological standpoint of the scholar — and, it must be stressed, the vision of history which this implies.

For those who view in a broadly positive light the reforming thrust of the 1931–3 governments, the fate of the Republic is to be explained by the underlying polarization within Spanish society, the inevitable conflicts which democracy therefore released, the obduracy of the conservative and the privileged, and the unwillingness of the main party of the right, the CEDA, to accept the Republic and the readjustment of wealth necessary to make democracy work. Left-wing militancy and more especially the leftward lurch of the Socialist Party are thus seen as responses to rightwing intransigence, and the right as bearing the main responsibility for political breakdown, ever-worsening social conflict, and ultimately, civil war. Critics of this view variously suggest that Socialist propensity to 'violence' anticipated that of the right; that unnecessary enemies for the Republic were created by anticlericalism and, in general, too narrow a view on the part of the left as to what constituted acceptable 'Republican' values, credentials and behaviour; and that the CEDA, a potentially Christian Democratic party which might have evolved in a genuinely democratic direction, was actually forced rightwards by the conduct of the left.

What these debates clearly indicate is the enormous potential for social and political conflict in the Spain of the 1930s, where a new democracy found itself, amid difficult economic circumstances and in an ideologically polarized Europe, grappling simultaneously with intricate political changes and pressing social problems. Notions of 'responsibility' are difficult to detach from personal views as to the urgency of reform and the reasonableness or otherwise of conservative resistance and lower-class impatience. To suggest that things might have been otherwise had important individuals or groups behaved differently is to ignore the situation within which they were acting, their perceptions of it and the traditions within which their outlook had been formed. 'Inevitable' is a word that historians should use sparingly, if at all, in relation to complex historical phenomena such as the failure and collapse of political regimes; suffice it to say therefore that in the case of the Spanish Republic failure was always more likely than survival.

Why did Franco win the Civil War?

Democracies, of course, often collapse without producing civil wars. In Spain, civil war exploded in 1936 owing to the roughly equal popular support commanded by the two sides, the rebels' failure to achieve a swift victory, the Republic's arming of the union militias, and — crucially — the fascist powers' intervention on the Nationalists' side. A war of years' rather than months' duration was then ensured by the Soviet Union's rallying to the Republic's aid.

Most writers agree that once the Civil War was under way, its outcome depended upon the manner in which, on the two sides, foreign aid and influence related to internal political and military considerations. Military and economic historians continue to argue about the quantities and quality of aid received by the two sides, and the financial and economic costs thereof. These were probably not, however, the deciding factors. Quantities apart, it is clear that while Soviet aid to the Republic was principally calculated to prolong resistance, Axis help for Franco was aimed successfully at victory. When to this is added the betrayal of the Republic by its supposed fellow democracies and the sorry farce of non-intervention, the Nationalists' advantage is clear and, by historians, little disputed.

A similar scholarly consensus exists over the Nationalists' vastly greater success in dealing with internal factionalism. When it comes to the internal politics of Republican Spain, however, disagreement abounds. The most intense, at times even bitter, debates have surrounded the question of Soviet aid to the Republic — its political and, therefore, military cost. Their starting point is, of course, the Republic's inability from late July 1936 to obtain help from elsewhere. As the price of its support the Soviet Union, in the interests of its own foreign policy, required the dismantling of revolutionary changes, conventional rather than guerrilla or 'revolutionary' war, the restoration of Republican authority and a massive enhancement of Communist power. While few serious historians have defended Communist excesses, some have argued that it was only the strategy in whose name they were committed that enabled the Republic to fight on for as long as it did.

The sharpest criticisms of this approach have been made — as they were at the time — from extreme left-wing but non-Stalinist positions. The Soviet Union, these critics argue, was uninterested in Republican victory and unwilling to provide sufficient resources to make it possible; to make matters worse, the anti-revolutionary policies and generally repressive conduct of the Communists, by robbing much of the population within Republican Spain of anything for which to fight, brought about massive demoralization and weakened rather than strengthened the bases of the anti-fascist struggle. In order to defeat an enemy who was always likely to be stronger in conventional military terms, the argument continues, what was required was a revolutionary war based upon a social transformation which as well as enthusing the population of Republican Spain might also have inspired to revolution that of the enemy zone.

The negative criticisms of Communist strategy and conduct are largely valid, though implicit in them is — or ought to be — an even greater criticism of the Anglo-French policies that deprived the Republic of aid save from a Soviet regime whose diplomatic over-tures the British and French governments spurned. Nevertheless, it seems highly improbable that had it been pursued the 'revolu-tionary' alternative, deprived as it would have been of *any* signifi-cant outside help, would have proved any more successful. Either of two sets of conditions might have brought the Spanish Civil War to a very different end: an immediate rallying of support from the Republic's fellow democracies, or Soviet assistance for a broad-based, revolutionary war rather than a sectarian, conventional one. In the climate of the 1930s, neither was remotely likely.

Francoism and fascism

During the 1930s the words 'fascism' and 'fascist' were so much in vogue as to make inevitable their widespread application to the Nationalist cause and the emergent Franco regime. While the words may have played little part in Nationalist propaganda, and the ideas they connoted have been uncongenial to many Catholics and erstwhile liberal monarchists within the Nationalist camp, nevertheless the prominence of the Falange and the involvement of Italy and Germany sufficed to satisfy most foreign observers, and by no means only those on the left, that the Spanish rebels were indeed 'fascists'. During the past twenty years, however, 'fascism' has become the object of rigorous academic analysis, with the result that much effort has been expended in attempting to establish whether or not the label *is* appropriate in the Spanish case.

The majority of historians have approached the problem via a definition of fascism based upon the radical-nationalist ideas and distinctive 'style' of the Italian model. Their perfectly logical conclusions are that the Falange and its predecessor the JONS were the only unambiguously fascist organizations in pre-Civil War Spain; that the CEDA in particular did not deserve the epithet 'fascist'; that after a sudden expansion during 1936 the Falange was politically neutered in April 1937 through its enforced merger with Carlism and the Catholic right; and that the subsequent regime, utterly dominated by the non-Falangist Franco, was therefore not fascist — whatever else it may have been.

Critics of this approach, while often accepting the usefulness of the Italian model in relation to Spain, have taken as their starting point the varied character of the Italian Fascist movement, its role as the militant defender of property and destroyer of the left, and the essential, rather than the external, characteristics of the Italian Fascist regime. This leads them to conclude that between 1931 and 1936 the Spanish right *as a whole* played a role analogous to that of fascism in Italy a decade earlier. Differences of ideology and programme within the right, they insist, were little greater than those within Italian fascism and in any case mattered little to thousands of right-wing militants, supporters and voters. What *was* important was a shared antagonism towards democracy and the left and a common commitment to some sort of authoritarian, corporate state. Leftists and Republicans were therefore entitled to feel that whether the right as a whole, or merely one element of it, achieved power, the consequences for them were likely to be more or less equally unpleasant. If the pre-1936 right can thus be considered 'objectively' fascist, it obviously follows that the same is true of the wartime alliance that emerged from it and of the Franco regime forged after October 1936.

Of these two approaches, the first has the virtue of identifying differences of ideology which were unquestionably important to some members of each right-wing party and were later to influence the internal politics of the Franco regime. Nevertheless, the second surely comes closer to reflecting the realities and passions of the 1930s. For the hundreds of thousands of Spanish — and non-Spanish — democrats and leftists who fought and died in the Civil War or in the horrendous repression that followed, the forces against which they struggled differed in few essentials from those that had recently brought dictatorship and oppression to Italy, Germany and Austria. If 'fascism' appeared to them an appropriate name for their enemy, then perhaps comfortable historians half-a-century later should hesitate before declaring them wrong.

Suggested Further Reading

Place of publication is London unless otherwise stated; ★ denotes paperback.

Anyone interested in Spain during the 1930s and the long-term background of the Civil War should read Gerald Brenan's classic work *The Spanish Labyrinth* (Cambridge University Press, 1943)★. The most satisfactory, though now somewhat dated, general history of Spain between 1931 and 1939 is Gabriel Jackson's *The Spanish Republic and the Civil War* (Princeton University Press, 1965)★. Two brief and fascinating illustrated histories of the Civil War are by Paul Preston, *The Spanish Civil War 1936–39* (Weidenfeld & Nicolson, 1986) and Gabriel Jackson, *A Concise History of the Spanish Civil War* (Thames & Hudson, 1974)★. Hugh Thomas, *The Spanish Civil War* (Penguin, 1977)★ is a monumental, immensely readable, largely narrative account of the Civil War. Perhaps, however, the most satisfying single-volume study of the war is Raymond Carr, *The Civil War in Spain* (Weidenfeld & Nicolson, 1986)★. Ronald Fraser, *Blood of Spain* (Allen Lane, 1979)★ is a quite superb oral history of the conflict.

Of the numerous more specialized works dealing with the period of the Second Republic and the Civil War, only a selection can be mentioned here. Paul Preston, *The Coming of the Spanish Civil War* (Methuen, 1983)★ and Richard A. H. Robinson, *The Origins of Franco's Spain* (David & Charles, 1970), deal in very different ways with left-right polarization between 1931 and 1936. Stanley G. Payne, *Falange: A History of Spanish Fascism* (Stanford University Press, 1961)★ and Martin Blinkhorn, *Carlism and Crisis in Spain, 1931–1939* (Cambridge University Press, 1975), cover the extreme right. Agrarian problems are discussed in Edward Malefakis' *Agrarian Reform and Peasant Revolution in Spain* (Yale University Press, 1970). The best available biography of Franco is J. P. Fusi, *Franco* (Macmillan, 1987). Gaston Leval, *Collectives in the Spanish Revolution* (Freedom Press, 1975)★ is an important anarchist account of the social revolution within Republican Spain; the communist destruction of that revolution is analysed in Burnett Bolloten, *The Spanish Revolution* (University of North Carolina Press, 1979)★. Among the many books dealing with foreign intervention and non-intervention, see Jill Edwards, *Britain and the Spanish Civil War* (Macmillan, 1979) and John F. Coverdale, *Italian Intervention in the Spanish Civil War* (Princeton University Press, 1977).

Memoirs and eye-witness accounts of the Civil War are legion. See in particular George Orwell, *Homage to Catalonia* (Gollancz, 1938; [Penguin ★]) and Arturo Barea's trilogy *The Forging of a Rebel* (Fontana, 1984)★.